Drew Plunkett

Drawing for Interior Design

Published in 2009
by Laurence King Publishing Ltd
361–373 City Road
London EC1V 1LR
Tel +44 20 7841 6900
Fax +44 20 7841 6910
E enquiries@laurenceking.com
www.laurenceking.com

A catalogue record for this book is available from the British Library

ISBN 978 185669 622 7
Designed by John Round Design
Printed in China

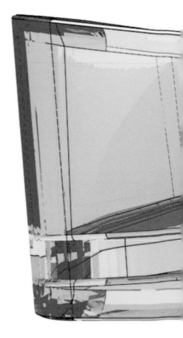

Drew Plunkett

Drawing for Interior Design

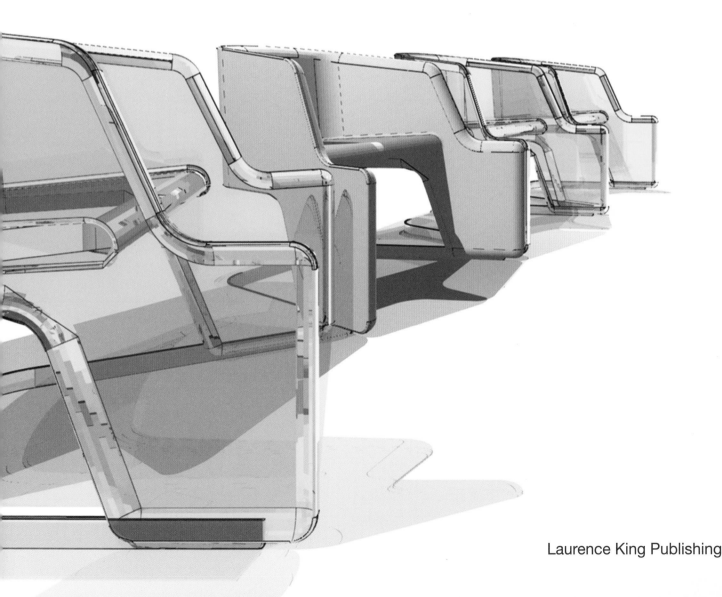

Laurence King Publishing

Contents

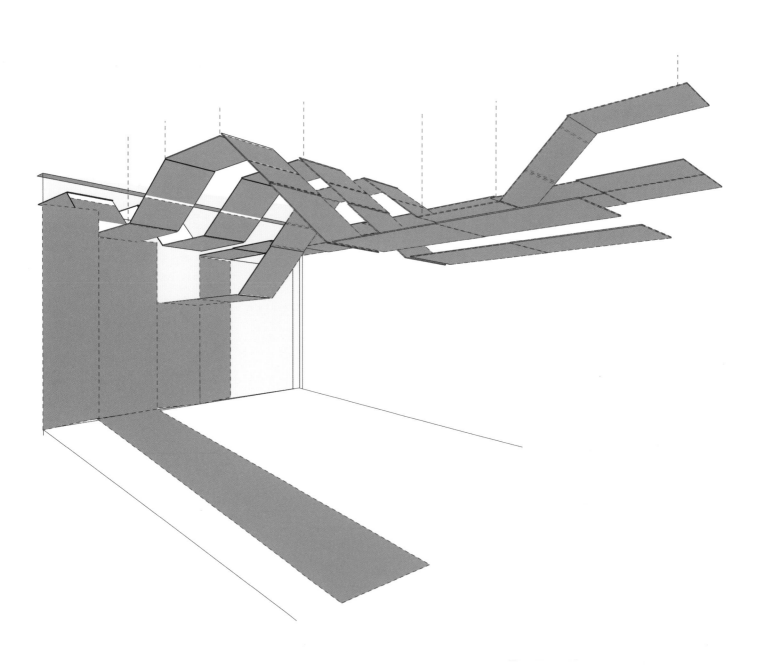

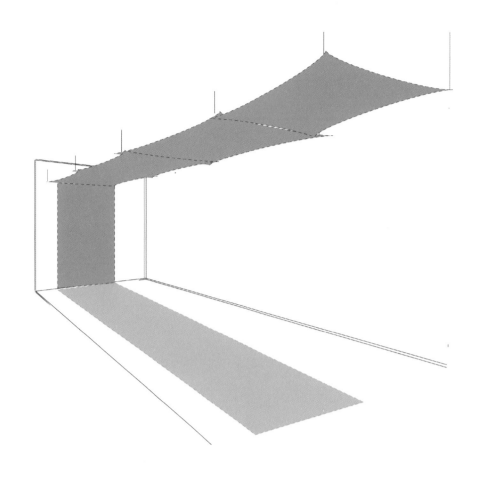

Introduction

Why we draw

Good interior design does not begin with a drawing but with an idea, an ill-defined image that exists for a moment in the imagination and continues to flit, evasively, across the mind's eye. Designing is, in effect, the pursuit of that image: a succession of attempts to define it more precisely, to give it form, to examine it and assess its worth, to make progressively more objective decisions that finalize ideas and to communicate those ideas to clients in the form of drawings and to builders in the form of instructions.

Drawing, at first speculatively and then precisely to scale, is the means to test most rigorously how a near-abstract concept can be viably translated into reality. It may be feasible to visualize and scrutinize these concepts without drawing them, but it would be perverse to deny that the most immediate and effective way to design is to make drawings – and drawings may take many forms. They do not have to be, perhaps should no longer be, handmade pen or pencil lines on conventional papers. They should be made in the way with which each individual designer is most comfortable. They should change to suit the particular requirements of each project. They are a means to the end of expressing ideas. Content should be more crucial than technique or style, which will take care of themselves.

As a designer becomes more experienced, making a drawing, the right kind of drawing, becomes automatic, instinctive, an immediate expression of thought. It need not be carefully refined but it does seem that when one is

Above
A computer-generated conceptual drawing, in which lines and blocks of colour are augmented by scanned artefacts and textures.

Above right
Most interiors depend for their success on two- rather than three-dimensional gestures. The computer allows the essence of these to be represented accurately and convincingly, with a little added drama.

Right
A hand drawing scanned and 'colour-washed' by computer.

intensely focused, absorbed in thinking about possibilities, and when the imagination and eye are practised, then the drawings produced have a quality that gives them a particular character and authority. Whatever kind of proposal is being made, effective and successful drawing helps build self-confidence and confidence in the ideas one is proposing – and it establishes credibility with clients.

The act of drawing gives structure both to thinking and to the coherent progression of ideas. Its particular potency is recognized in the caveat that one should delay making the first drawing in order to allow ideas to float freely in the imagination. This warning acknowledges that once the abstraction of thought is given shape, wide-ranging speculation comes to an end, and the identity of the project and the direction of its evolution are as good as settled. Every designer experiences that moment of frustration when

a fruitless idea is obsessively and repetitively committed to paper, as if the hand is stubbornly denying the imagination the chance to move on. At times like that the only way to progress is to stop drawing and to think, to allow the imagination the chance to start again.

In effect, all drawings but the final one made in the course of developing a project have some shortcomings. All are made in the optimistic expectation that they will encapsulate a final solution, but under objective scrutiny all except the last – while they may offer some encouraging evidence of progress – will be found wanting. It is the identification of their shortcomings that will further inform not only the direction that the design process should follow but also the questions being asked in the brief, for these become inevitably more modified and complex as one begins to understand how the realities of an existing

Above
Detailed description of the relationship between new and existing structures is much easier to create by computer. In addition, the image – generated from plans and sections – may be rotated on-screen for selection of the best viewpoint.

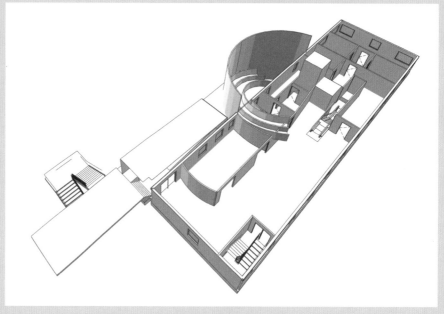

Above left
The earliest sketches represent a designer's first attempts to give physical form to what must inevitably be unresolved ideas. Further refinement requires more precise representation and investigation.

Above
Drawings made to scale clarify precisely the interaction of elements within the project and allow final decisions to be made about proportions. Simple three-dimensional images, generated on computer, also help clients understand the composition and organization of a project.

building determine what is possible. The client's perceptions must also change as the nature of what is possible changes. The contribution and agreement of the client is essential for the progression of any project, and the reasons for decision-making must be communicated to them clearly. Appropriate, well-made drawings are the most effective way of doing this.

Making a good drawing requires practice and an understanding of how that drawing may best convey information. While all drawings, like everything a designer produces, should aspire to be beautiful their first obligation is to convey information, and ultimately their success must be judged on their capacity to do this. Ideas need to be assessed objectively, regardless of the quality of the drawing that describes them. However, it is not unreasonable to suggest that when a good idea emerges it will generate a good drawing – one that is likely to capture the essence of an idea, in this case the atmosphere of an interior, as much as it defines practical realities.

Different stages in the design process require different kinds of drawing. As the design becomes more precisely defined so the drawings become more exact; while initial sketches may be flamboyant and suggestive of an intense involvement with the creative moment, they are, because of their very spontaneity, more superficial than the prosaic plans, elevations and details that follow and explain in detail how the building will be made. It is in these precisely scaled drawings, showing little evidence of graphic gestures, that the designer becomes increasingly engaged with the reality of their proposal, the imagination is most intensely engaged and distractions are least intrusive

The tools and materials with which designers make their drawings have always been in a state of evolution and the capacities of particular media have, inevitably, had an impact on the way designers 'see' their ideas and influenced how they, and others, appraise them. It is comparatively recently that the sedate evolution of the pencil, pen and felt tip has been crucially interrupted.

The impact of the computer

There is still some disagreement about whether images produced by computer can be described as 'drawings' at all. Those who harbour doubts have a visceral feeling that a drawing is something that must be made by the hand and that the communion of hand, eye and intellect has a power which offers the only true road to visual creativity.

There is a sentimental presumption that drawing by hand represents a more 'artistic' activity than drawing by computer, but this is an argument usually put forward by those with a vested interest in their own well-developed and polished drafting skills. It also denies the evidence of history. The pencil on paper is an improvement on the stick that scratched lines in the mud and sand, and on the quill that dripped ink onto parchment. It made possible a better

standard of drawing and added to the capacity of those making drawings to express themselves more effectively. The computer does the same, but even more dramatically.

The computer, although it has only been widely used in the field of interior design for a little over ten years, has become the drawing tool of choice. This is because it is the most effective instrument available to support the practice of interior design, and the material it produces is inherently compatible with the new and ubiquitous digital mechanisms of global communication. It is becoming progressively more easy to use, and such development is likely to continue as long as producers of hardwares and softwares compete to offer more user-friendly – and, therefore, from their point of view – commercially successful options.

Top left
The computer has now become the drawing tool of choice for interior designers.

Top right
The computer offers complex and complementary options for the rendering of three-dimensional images.

Above
The computer can introduce the extraordinary into the depiction of the (comparatively) ordinary.

While the extravagant claims of the early supporters of computers – that the machines would take over the creative process – have gone unrealized, and are likely to remain so, the more modest reality is that they have had a fundamental impact on how people now engage with the process of creating interiors. Qualities that are essential in the making of a good interior – lighting, colour, texture, transparency and reflectivity – are all extremely difficult, some nearly impossible, to represent with traditional manual techniques. However, using computers it is comparatively simple to represent these essentials with a great – even sometimes unsettling – degree of realism. Designers trained, and variously adept, in the use of manual techniques have been reluctantly compelled to acknowledge that the computer does those jobs better than they ever could.

The fears that computer imaging would force uniformity of visualizing, and of the consequent built output, have been allayed by the evidence. The new medium has added to the creative palette, enabling rather than stifling creativity and diversity. It is possible to make both good and bad drawings by either hand or computer. Relative merit is the result of refined technique and taste. A critical eye, rather than the computer or the hand, is what makes a drawing good.

The fear that all drawings made on computer and all interiors built from these would look the same has therefore been dispatched, but there is a generic look to computer-generated images. There is, of course, also a generic look to those made by hand and, just as with handmade drawings, the more one practises and perfects the use of appropriate software so the more distinctly individual the computer-generated image becomes. The maxim that applied to traditional drawing, that the identity of the maker was always clear in a good drawing and that all bad drawings shared an anonymous and unattributable ineptitude, is equally true for those made by computer. The mechanical, dispassionate and unadventurous implementation of instructions in a software manual will offer only the most prosaic description of reality, but the evidence would suggest that for every designer, regardless of the quality of creative design work, the lowest level of digital drawing will be significantly more acceptable than that of an incompetent hand drawing.

Designers who use software creatively offer themselves, and others, the chance to consider a richer, more accurate and informative representation of their ideas. If one accepts

Above left and left
The computer-made image is the most effective way of representing materiality and atmosphere.

Above
This image concentrates on the dominant elements in the space – the products and display – focusing on them as the eye would and only hinting at elements of the existing building, which are of secondary importance.

Right
Crucial construction details are
identified, considered in two
dimensions at a small scale (1:50 or
1:20), then drawn at 1:5 or full size
with explanatory technical notes.
Often when, as in this example,
the construction process is
complex and ground-breaking, the
final stage will involve discussion
with specialist consultants and
manufacturers.

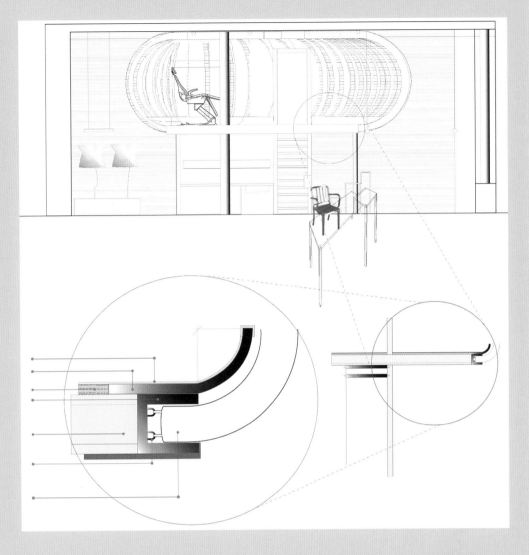

that the opinions of a client are an essential element in the
evolution of a successful project, then the more clearly and
precisely ideas are represented the more productive the
dialogue will be.

If computers significantly extend the possibilities of
exploring and communicating the physicality of a proposal,
so they have hugely impacted on the making of production
drawings that provide builders with the information they
need to construct the designer's intentions. They ensure
drawings of extraordinary precision, to which text may be
added without the laborious tedium of stencilling and in
which the inevitable changes that become necessary as the
project evolves may be seamlessly incorporated.

Compatibility of drawing software with information
and communication technologies enables instant global
distribution of drawings and an exchange of ideas that
wholly supersedes the efficiency of any postal service,
making creative collaboration with specialist consultants and
manufacturers simpler and more spontaneous. Problems on
a site half the world away can be digitally photographed
and sent instantly to the designer, who may identify and

communicate a solution just as rapidly. One reservation may
be that the possibility, and perceived obligation, to reply
quickly will discourage the extended consideration that a
critical problem might require.

Computer basics

Most drawing softwares offer a reasonable quality of three-dimensional image, capable of meeting almost all requirements for developing and presenting ideas. However, in creating the most polished and realistic images it is often necessary to use a combination of programs, and, just as images made on different hardwares and softwares can appear very similar (as do drawings made by hand), so the basic steps in creating them are essentially the same. Two examples demonstrate this: one, on the left, by Richard

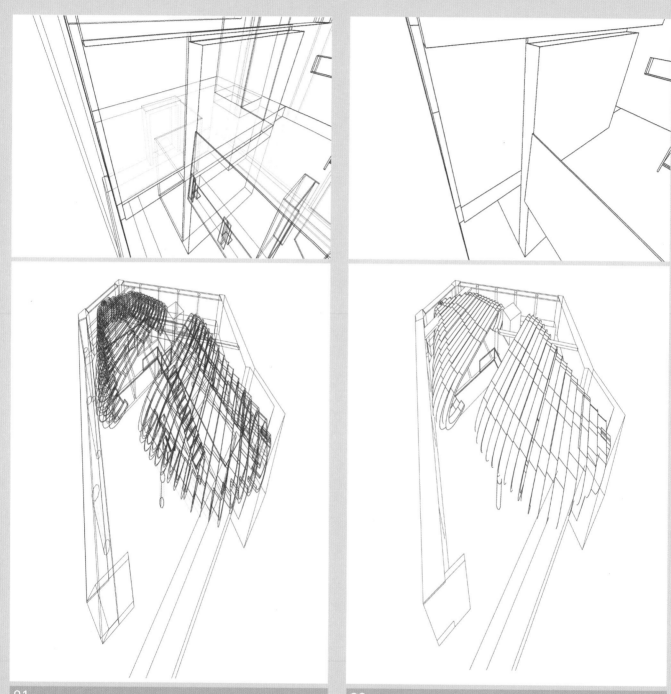

01
In the first step – the 'wire frame' – all lines generated by the projection of plan and section are visible.

02
The 'hidden' lines – those obscured by the planes of walls, floor, ceiling and other solids – are eliminated to provide the first clear three-dimensional 'model' of the space.

Smith is primarily concerned with representing materials;
the other, on the right, by Olga Valentinova Reid with
representing form. Each uses different hardware and a
combination of different softwares.

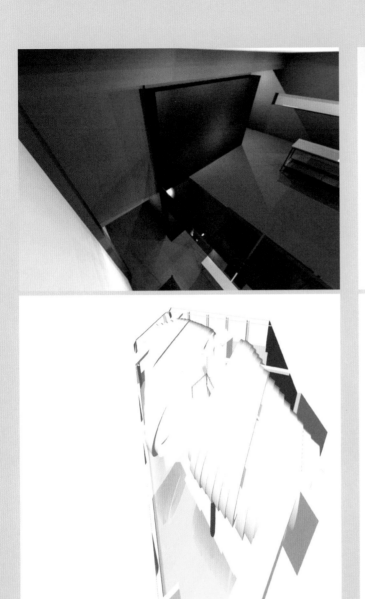

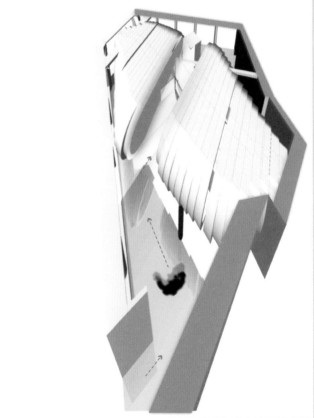

03
The first renderings of materials, textures and lighting are added. This stage
allows an appraisal to be made of the composition of the image.

04
The lighting and materiality are fine-tuned.

We are not, in this book, considering the particular merits of different software packages. Most of the specialist programs fulfil the essential requirements satisfactorily. Each is in a fairly constant state of flux, developing more useful additions to a basic repertoire and creating often strikingly familiar versions of successful rival softwares. It is therefore increasingly easy, particularly as software interfaces become simpler to use, to move from one program to another. Comparisons of images made with different softwares, and combinations between packages, indicate that all can achieve a comparable level of refinement.

Those who first used computers in design practice were not only learning an unfamiliar way of working but grappling with equipment that was significantly more difficult to use than current (and, presumably, future) versions. They were also trying to disengage from the habits of drawing by hand,

having to organize the way they put a drawing together in unfamiliar ways. Cumbersome early programs, untested in the fields of practice, did perhaps require a significant degree of induction and dedicated experience of use, but it would now be a short-sighted employer who would reject a talented designer on the grounds that they were unfamiliar with the practice's preferred software (although this may continue to be a useful diplomatic way of rejecting an unsuitable applicant).

Any good interior-design school should now be inducting students into the use of computers at the beginning of the course, allowing them to find and evolve their own way of thinking through this essential tool. Just as one should not be aware of the pencil in one's hand when drawing, so, ideally, one should not have to deliberate over procedures for making an appropriate computer image.

This page
The basic three-dimensional images for these three projects were generated by different software programs and refined using further specialist softwares to import textures, materials, furniture and figures.

The essential skill in making an effective drawing, particularly one that attempts to represent an interior realistically, is to be able to visualize it accurately in one's imagination – the same skill that was necessary to make a good drawing by hand. Because the image in the designer's 'eye' is the crucial ingredient in determining the 'look' of a drawing, there is likely to be more variation in the work of two individuals using the same program than in two drawings by the same designer on two different software programs.

The following pairs of drawings show how the computer makes possible the production of images that are distinctly different but that complement the style of the projects they illustrate.

When experienced designers have polished their computer-imaging skills, it becomes impossible to attempt to identify the programs they use and the impact of these on their work. Designers' individual ways of seeing become the determining factor in the expression of ideas. Rather than forcing graphic conformity as was, and is still sometimes, argued, the computer makes possible an extraordinary diversity of image. Examples on these pages – each pair is the work of one designer – demonstrate this.

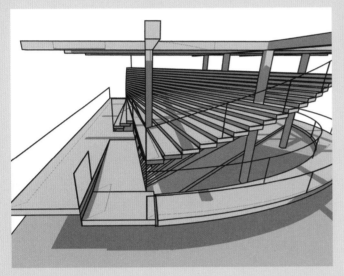

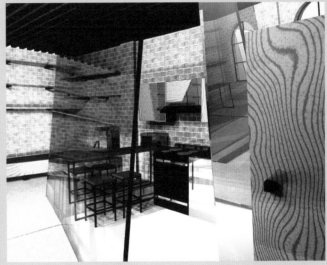

Above and above right
The limitations of hand skills do not allow such extreme diversity of expression.

Below and below right
The unique character of each proposal is distinctively represented, and complex detail convincingly realized.

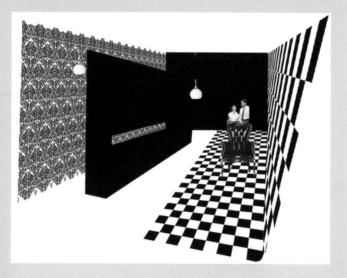

Left and far left
In the work of designers who
are experienced at working
with computers it is sometimes
impossible to identify which
programs have been used – it is
the designers' ways of seeing that
become the determining factor in
the expression of ideas, rather than
the software itself.

Above right and above
The particular 'eye' of each
designer is clear in both of
these very different images. The
computer does not eliminate the
individual mark.

Far left and left
Diverse and unconventional
images such as these confound
arguments that computers lead to
graphic conformity.

The future

The often embarrassing history of predictions about future technologies suggests that any speculation that is too dogmatic is largely futile. The extraordinarily rapid development of computer-generated visualization suggests that the activity will continue to change significantly, but it is perhaps possible to speculate about the likely direction of emerging software and hardware.

It is likely that the potential and operation of programs will increasingly converge as professional preferences and priorities become clearer. Operating systems are likely to become increasingly compatible. Potentially the most exciting change is the refinement of digital drawing pads with the digital conversion of 'freehand' sketches into precise 'technical' drawings for builders on site.

As computer-aided manufacture (CAM) develops, its capacity to relate to computer-aided design (CAD) instructions will become increasingly streamlined and refined. Techniques presently used successfully in mass manufacturing and occasional batch production will be tuned to meet the inevitably one-off nature of interior elements. The software and machinery used in rapid prototyping (the construction of scaled three-dimensional facsimiles) and laser cutting (the hyper accurate cutting of complex forms out of or into the surface of sheet materials) is already proving a cost-effective way of making three-dimensional models and both these techniques are adaptable to full-size production.

Drawing programs increasingly allow designers to conceptualize in three-dimensional images, which can be converted automatically into two-dimensional plans and sections, essential to achieve the precision necessary to finalize plans and details to meet practical requirements. It is conceivable that once data relative to plans and sections of an existing building shell is fed into the computer, along with appropriate anthropometric and ergonomic material, then appropriate software might determine which design speculations were viable, so that two-dimensional checking forms an integral part of three-dimensional investigation.

The computer's capacity to create animated 'walk-throughs' of interiors is an established, if expensive, presentation option. It can be initially spectacular but is compromised. Spectators' experience of movement through the space, particularly if the sequence is viewed on a monitor screen, is limited, and the images lack the three-dimensional depth of a physical model. This latter problem may be overcome by digital projection at a large scale, which makes interpretation easier for spectators unfamiliar with reading drawn images, and, increasingly, by the development of the software and hardware that generates three-dimensional images with perceived depth. Ultimately success will depend on the refinement of the representation of materials within the images and on the ease by which spectators control their movement through the interior. Ideally, the image should respond to the direction of the spectator's gaze. Once the visual refinement is achieved it will be desirable to complete the sensory repertoire by adding sound and sensations of touch, and perhaps even, when warranted, smell.

Something more extraordinary than these suggestions, as yet unanticipated, will materialize. Those who learnt and matured as designers in pre-digital times will inexorably fade away and ways of visualizing and, therefore, thinking about interiors will change. The creative process for interior designers is not about how you draw but what you draw and the more effective tools will inevitably prevail.

As designers refine and become more intensely involved with the development of a project, so the nature of the drawings they make to describe it often take on a particular identity that is singularly appropriate to the underpinning concept. Such drawings are often the most effective way of communicating, perhaps subliminally, the spirit of a project to a client. These two drawings by Yoshi Sugimoto demonstrate not only that creative use of computer imaging allows the individual designer to use, with equal facility, distinctly different drawing styles, but that these can be inspired by and complementary to the spirit of the project itself. Both drawings are intended to explain the concept that underpins each project and their originality suggests a creative confidence that has grown from the designer's immersion in the design process and taken him a long way beyond the obvious first solutions.

Right

The same trompe l'oeil pattern used on the ceiling of the lower level and floor of the upper, dominates the image as it would the built interior. Single-point perspective is employed independently on each level, but the combination of two viewpoints adds ambiguity to the image and greater significance to the trompe l'oeil illusion. Each level demonstrates variations on shared themes: star patterns on similar but different padded backgrounds – each decorated with an incongruous item of clothing, the hemispherical chairs, resting on the floor above and hanging from the ceiling below, the silhouettes of animals and birds. The stars floating on the edges of the drawing repeat an important decorative motif and help give the illusion of depth. Both black and white figures emphasize the mirroring of planes.

Opposite

In this example the conceptual essence of the project again determines the nature of the drawing. The interior of a simple cellular structure is made extraordinary by an eclectic collection of elements, all of which, including wall finishes, are crucial in establishing the character of each level. Each object is set, with equal status, against a shared black background to establish its individual character, while the specification notes attached to each emphasize their normality and accessibility. The colours of the figures, which give scale and explain the function of each level, complement and augment those of the levels they inhabit. The image of the moon relates to the building's function as a predominantly nocturnal place.

perspective

Models

There is one crucial area of the design process for which, at present, neither the handmade or computer drawing offers the most effective tool, and that is the representation of complex volumes. The hand labours to define perspectives accurately and, while the computer can achieve that as effortlessly as it delineates two dimensions, it consistently 'flattens' the volumes contained between walls, floors and ceilings. A real, rather than a virtual, three-dimensional model conveys the potential reality of complex three-dimensional space more effectively and, since we are here discussing essential visualizing tools, it is legitimate to

acknowledge and discuss physical model-making.

Such models need not be meticulously constructed. They may be made quickly, and roughly, like a drawn sketch. They can be torn apart and reconfigured in minutes but, like the sketch, will have conviction if their maker has become adept through sustained practice and their contribution to discussion is useful.

Left
A model which has been amended a number of times during the design process is still useful as a means of describing to a client the three-dimensional intentions of a project.

Below left
A finished model provides a comprehensive explanation of how the elements of a complex interior work together. In this example, the relationship of the interior to the levels of the street is clearly explained. The figures give scale.

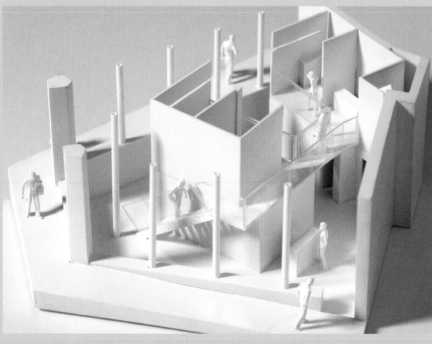

About this book

This book concentrates on describing why drawings are made, and the techniques and qualities that go into making good drawings. Any drawing technique can only improve with sustained, self-critical practice. In addition, one learns from others not only how they have made successful drawings but also why they have made them. The interior designer must be able to create a number of quite different types of drawing, each with its own conventions, which are the result of well-tried and tested experience. These may usefully be narrowed down in favour of a uniform final approach, but it is counterproductive to reject these early variations arbitrarily.

Much of the discussion in this book about drawing deals, inevitably, with the nature of the design process. This is not to trespass into other territories but rather to recognize that the act of drawing – in two or three dimensions, by hand or computer – is so intimately a part of thinking about design that the two must be discussed as one.

The book makes suggestions about how drawings and models can be made most effectively by hand, but it does not attempt to explain how to use particular computer programs. These are in a constant state of development and refinement, and instruction is most effectively and comprehensively found for each in its relevant manual.

Every designer has an individual way of drawing and making, which is as distinct as their handwriting. It is something that emerges from personal ability and individual preference but, broadly speaking, it will be shaped by personal variations on a universal battery of skills and techniques that have been proven in professional practice. The final manifestation of the ideas has to do with personal preferences and, inevitably, style of drawing will tend to reflect the style of interior produced. Those who make flamboyant gestures within their interiors tend to draw flamboyantly, avoiding technical precision as long as possible – often longer than is productive. Others will move quickly to a precise definition of their proposal, and may miss out on some of the unpredictable ideas that a less controlled exploration might reveal. However, since it is easier to build straight lines and right angles the more controlled technique is more likely to result in the more realizable building. Elaborate, complex forms require more money because they are more difficult to build, and usually, if they are to be successful, require more effort from the designer for the same fee as a more conventional project.

There appears to be a clear correlation between the success of designers' work and the rigour of their working methods. Natural talent can only be expressed if it is backed by intense hard work. It is not difficult to have an idea, but it is very difficult to convert that intangible thought into a built reality.

The computer makes the production of drawings a little more egalitarian than hand-drafting in that one does not need the same degree of inherent manual dexterity. However, the ability to create a wonderful building remains paramount, and perhaps there is a different pressure on the designer in that the content rather than the quality of the drawing now falls under greater scrutiny and credit is no longer given for the successful grind of producing a decent handmade drawing. The computer gives each individual a battery of techniques, with an almost guaranteed successful outcome. Polishing of skills requires individual commitment, but this book and the analysis of the drawings it contains offers examples that point to a diversity of rewarding directions for exploration.

About the drawings in this book

The drawings used in this book have been made in the creation, presentation and realization of projects, some by practitioners and some by students. Many of the designers are familiar with each others' work, and some of that work will demonstrate how collaboration can lead to productive cross-fertilization of ideas or, more importantly, how a shared idea is developed in a distinctly individual way by distinctly creative individuals.

It makes sense to look at the work of students, particularly for presentation drawings, because they have time to concentrate on the development of techniques and to push these to the limit in order to explain proposals that must, necessarily, remain on paper. Professionals make such drawings intermittently and are therefore less practised and less inclined to experiment, liable to fall back on familiar techniques and unable to devote time to exploring new directions. Students also tend to be more relaxed when working with computers and therefore more prone to experimentation. They have grown up with them as an integral part of their everyday lives.

Chapter 1
The Basics

The need for a measured survey

It is important when designing an interior, particularly one that involves complex subdivision of an existing space, to know the exact dimensions of that space because decisions about the location of new elements inevitably depend on the particularities of the original structure. While drawings of existing buildings may frequently be found and referred to, there are some for which no records exist, and others for which the drawings do not inspire confidence in their own accuracy. In such cases it therefore becomes necessary to carry out a measured survey and to produce an accurate version of plans, sections and significant details. Even for recently constructed buildings it is worth checking the accuracy of dimensions on drawings because variations and discrepancies almost inevitably occur, and go unrecorded, during the building process. A very small discrepancy can often cause problems and embarrassment.

When no drawings exist it is normal to draw a plan on site, usually by hand, and good practice to record systematically all measurements because until design work begins it is impossible to forecast those which are likely to be crucial in the decision-making process. If the general outcome can already be anticipated with confidence, then it may be safe to take selective measurements, although, almost invariably, something will be overlooked, and only in the making of the measured drawing will this become clear.

Carrying out a survey

It is good practice to take 'running' dimensions rather than measuring and recording each element separately. Running dimensions are made by measuring sequentially all significant points on, for example, a wall from one clearly identifiable point, usually a corner. This prevents the accumulative error that is likely to occur when a collection of separate dimensions are aggregated on a drawing. The running dimension effectively offers the opportunity for correction with each individual reading. This is vital, particularly as the conditions on most sites are unlikely to support meticulous accuracy. Buildings in use are likely to be cluttered with inconveniently placed furniture. Unoccupied shells tend to be badly lit and possibly littered with building equipment.

There are circumstances in which it is obvious that only a few isolated dimensions will be needed, and then it is enough to take a series of single measurements. This is also the easier method when working alone.

It is, however, better if two people collaborate to make a survey: one to hold the end of a long measuring tape and record, on the plan, the dimensions called out by the second, who will move along the length of the wall. Over a long distance the tape, if held in the air, will sag, increasing measurements. It is good practice, when possible, to lay the tape along the floor. When this is impractical because of clutter, it may be sensible over a long distance to measure in two or more sections to reduce weight and sag.

It is always unwise to assume that corners are perfect right angles because although most will appear so to the eye this, particularly in the case of older buildings, is almost never the case. It is obviously important that angles are accurate and, to establish these, it is vital to measure the diagonals of surveyed spaces. A diagonal, together with the two walls it connects, represents the sides of a triangle, and when this is drawn to scale the angle of the intersection of the walls is established accurately.

It is easy to overlook diagonals, just as it is to forget about measuring heights. It is always necessary to have heights of ceilings, door and window heads, window cills, steps in floors and ceilings, the depth of beams and other dimensions particular to individual spaces. To distinguish these from horizontal dimensions on the drawing it is usual to draw a circle around them and, as far as possible, place them separately from horizontal dimensions.

There are usually places in any building where a lot of dimensions must be recorded and it is better to draw these areas to a larger scale so that the new drawing has enough space to accommodate the density of information.

It is advisable to try to make the accurately scaled

drawing based on the survey findings as quickly as possible, while the realities of the site are fresh in the memory. It is always sensible to take photographs of a space, and particularly of complex areas or details. Digital photography makes prolific record-making easy.

It is sensible to assume that a second surveying visit may be necessary to check discrepancies and correct omissions, and it is diplomatic to warn an occupant or owner of the building of this probability. It is better to make this sound like a regular procedure than to appear to be correcting oversights.

Compact laser measures are increasingly replacing the traditional tape measuring tools and, with their inbuilt digital programming, they can also calculate areas and volumes. The most basic models can measure lengths up to 100 metres (328 feet) with an accuracy of plus or minus 1.5 mm (¹⁄₁₆ inch). Most have built-in spirit levels for horizontal alignment and project a light spot onto the surface defining the length measured, to avoid readings being made to inappropriate obstructions and projections. One person can carry out the survey, with no need to have the end of the tape held and measurements called out.

TIP MEASURING TOOLS

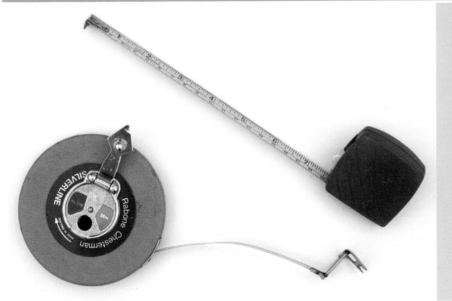

The bottom tape, typically made of canvas or flexible metal and 30 metres (150 feet) long, is used to take horizontal dimensions.

The top tape, typically 3 metres (10 feet) long and more rigid, is used to measure small spaces and heights.

A freehand plan of the space is made in a small sketchbook (see the left-hand page). While it is good if this is proportionately accurate, it may be distorted to allow more space on the page where a number of dimensions need to be recorded in a small area. In this case, the drawing does not register the angles that emerge when it is redrawn to scale (see page 74). Such discrepancies can be alarming when they first appear in the studio and it may be necessary, for peace of mind, to return to the site for confirmation. If, however, the survey has been comprehensively carried out and there are enough interacting dimensions then one may be confident that the angles are accurate.

The 'running' dimensions for each wall are normally taken from the left-hand corner as one looks at the wall. When necessary, widths of individual elements along the wall may be calculated by subtracting the left-hand dimension from the right. The diagonals are measured. Heights are recorded in circles to distinguish them from horizontal dimensions. A few parts of the drawing are shaded for clarification, for example the windows on the top right and, for clear identification, the column in the middle of the floor.

The column position is established on the ground floor by the distance of its centre point, measured at right angles, from two walls. It is important in this instance to indicate that the measurement is made from the wall and not the face of the projecting brick pier. The depth of the pier's projection is not recorded. It may be that since it is a brick pier, and constructed in accordance with the module of brick sizes, it was assumed that the dimension would be easily remembered and did not need recording. It is, however, more likely to be an oversight needing to be checked later – particularly if the pier has a critical relationship to the proposed new construction.

The plan on the right-hand page records, in particular, the location of high-level windows, overall dimensions of the walls having been determined by the data for the lower. The dotted-and-dashed line represents a beam overhead, and the note with it records its depth below the

ceiling. A wooden or metal rod, which will not flop over, is the appropriate tool for making vertical measurements.

The two plans in the bottom left of each page record dimensions for the door and window openings. These elements are likely to be unaffected by the project work but their accurate depiction on the plans and sections will give credibility to later drawings and remind the designer about the depth of reveals, which may well later play a part in decision-making about interior details.

There are projects, involving no new construction or where the location of new construction is already determined, for which the measurements needed can be anticipated accurately. In this example, on the right the few dimensions are enough to establish the position of an overhead beam towards the bottom of the drawing and the geometry of the bay window at the top.

When it is necessary to return to a site for additional information it will be very clear what this is and a few isolated dimensions will be enough. A return visit may not always be to take

additional measurements but could be to confirm that the plan drawn from the original notes is accurate. With complicated surveys there are often ambiguities and apparent discrepancies that demand to be checked.

The lower sketch records dimensions for a door frame, and because it is safe to assume that right angles would be cut very accurately for such an element, the dimensions shown are enough to establish the angle.

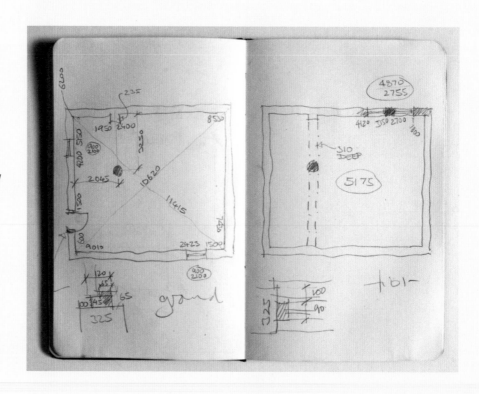

Opposite

A notebook with initial freehand survey drawings. The drawing on the left page records dimensions of walls and diagonal measurements. The drawing on the right page records dimensions relating to a column and brick pier on the ground floor of the space.

Right

A simple measurement sketch for a space where no new constuction is needed.

Below right

Sketch recording dimensions for a door frame.

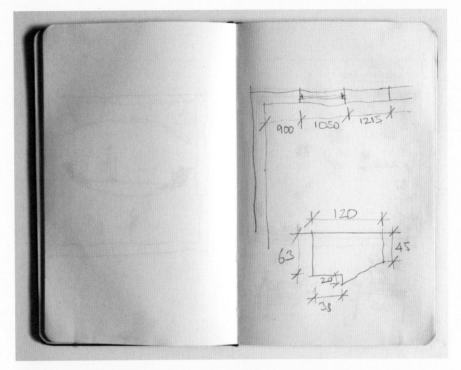

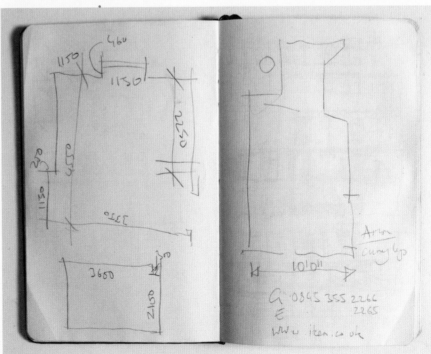

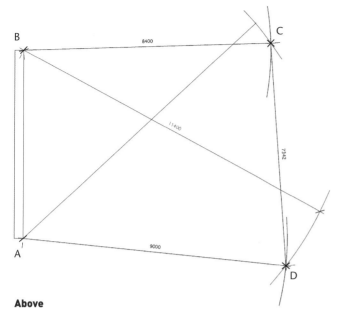

Above
An accurate scale sketch showing external wall dimensions.

Drawing a plan from survey information

All lines are drawn to scale. The wall between corners A and B is drawn vertically. (On computer it is easier to draw this as a box, representing the width of the wall, than to make the single lines of a handmade drawing.) The intersection of the arcs representing the length of the wall from B to C and the diagonal from A locate C. The intersection of the arcs representing the length of the walls from C to D and A to D locate D. The whole may be checked by plotting the diagonal from B, which should intersect corner D. This is unlikely to be wholly precise, since the measuring process is subject to error and the computer will make a scrupulously accurate interpretation of the data.

When the angles of the external walls have been established, the details of the plan may be added. The drawing uses established drawing conventions for doors and windows, and minor variations might be made to these as long as they broadly retain their recognized configurations. Too much variation and the drawings will fail to communicate effectively. The dotted-and-dashed line – the graphic indicator of elements higher than 1200 millimetres (4 feet) above floor level, at which height plans are conventionally drawn – represents the beam at ceiling level in the upper-level plan.

When an accurate record has been made of the existing building it is possible to begin the design process. Sections can be drawn using the information on plan and the heights from the survey notes.

The essential information about any project is communicated in a comprehensive set of plans and sections. The number of plans is determined by the number of floors but the number of sections depends on the nature of the proposal. The section's function is to explain the interaction between levels, and so a decision must be made about the appropriate number and where each 'cut' may most effectively be made. The location of the cut determines how much useful information the drawing will yield, and it is important to indicate its position on plans with a 'section line'.

The graphic interpretation of plans and sections is a matter of taste, and consideration should be given to their compatibility with the 'spirit' of the project. Whatever that decision may be, it is always sensible to distinguish new construction from old because this allows clients to see immediately the extent of the work envisaged. If no differentiation is made it is difficult for clients to identify the new work, and their cautious assumption tends to be that this constitutes more than it actually does – which in turn suggests greater cost.

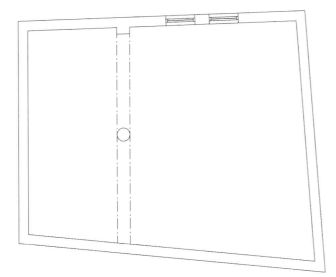
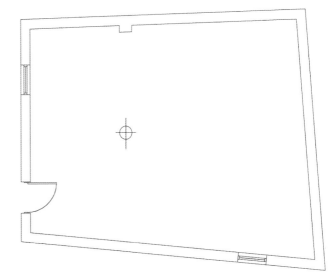

Above left and right

After establishing the angles of the external walls, details of internal walls, doors and windows are added. Dotted lines conventionally indicate elements higher than 1200 mm (47 inches) above floor level – in this case a ceiling beam.

TIP SECTION LINES

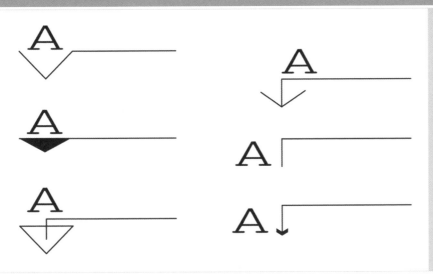

The section line, which indicates the location of the cut, need not be drawn continuously across the plan because additional lines can complicate the reading of those representing built elements. It is sufficient to indicate its position on the edge of the plan, but arrows at each end of it must indicate the orientation of the section. These arrows are good examples of how personal taste may influence the graphic style of a drawing. They may take any form as long as they are unambiguous.

Graphic options

The solution in the first vertical sequence (below left) is acceptable, and clearly distinguishes between old and new. However, the solid black of the existing structure tends to overpower the new work.

The modesty of the grey existing walls, and other elements, in the second sequence (below right) allows the yellow of the new walls to assert itself, and this is particularly useful in drawing attention to the slim new column.

The parity of old and new in the plans in the third sequence (opposite page, left) eliminates the distinction between them, but the tone added to new walls in the sections effectively makes the distinction – as does the heavier outline in the lowest drawing.

The fourth sequence (opposite page, right) is the

least successful because the hatching of the existing elements creates visual interference.

Nevertheless all the formulae shown work, to a greater or lesser extent. Any coding is acceptable as long as the drawing is easily understood, and to ensure this certain conventions must be observed.

Essential conventions

On the examples of the ground-floor plans, the dotted-and-dashed lines indicate the edge of the upper floor. On the first-floor plans the dashed line indicates the wall of the room below.

Plans are essentially horizontal sections nominally drawn at 1200 millimetres (4 feet) above floor level, which means that they cut through most windows and

Right
In this first sequence, a column of plans showing one way to indicate walls and existing elements by using solid filled lines, with new elements shown as lighter lines. The bottom sectional image shows the standard way to draw stairs.

Far right
In the second sequence, existing walls are shown as a paler shaded grey, to allow the new elements, in yellow, to stand out.

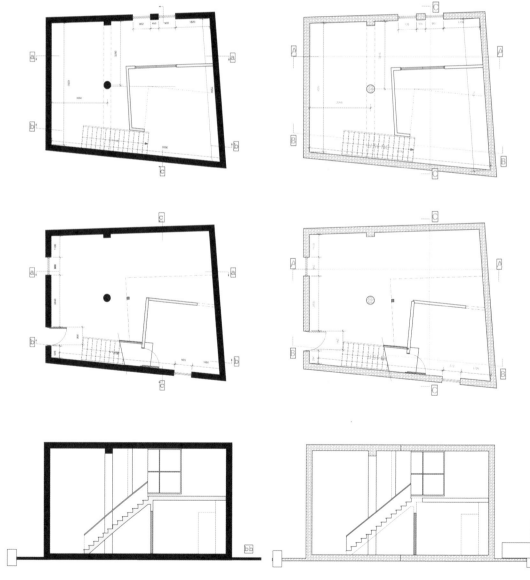

therefore include these crucial elements. A high-level window should be indicated with dotted-and-dashed lines, since its existence is likely to have a significant impact on design decisions.

It is worth noting the standard practice for drawing stairs. A stair, unless it is leading to a change of level less than 1200 millimetres (4 feet) above the main floor, is inevitably cut through and it is the convention that it be shown cut off, at an angle, at approximately 1200 millimetres (4 feet) above floor level. This allows some indication to be made of the construction below it: in this example, a store entered from within the room in the lower right-hand corner. An arrow always points towards the top of stairs. On upper floors, the entire stair is visible because it is below the level of the plan 'cut'.

Right
The distinction between existing and new elements in the third sequence has been lessened, though the tone added to the walls in the sections does make the distinction clear.

Far right
In the fourth sequence, existing elements are indicated by using hatching.

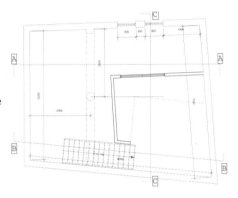

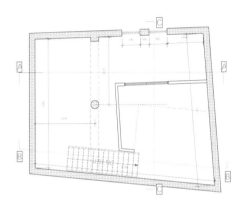

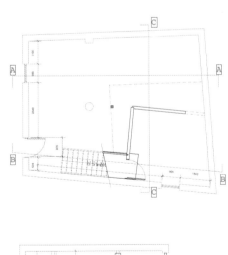

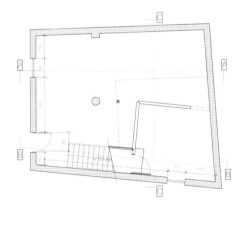

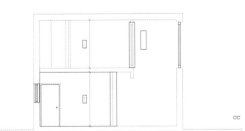

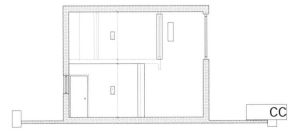

Moving to the third dimension

Once the plan and sectional information has been fed into the computer, it is then simple to generate convincing three-dimensional views that can, in turn, provide a basic form to which colours, textures and lighting may be added.

There are a range of standard three-dimensional projections, all of which the computer produces with equal ease.

While it is still possible to conform to traditional axonometric and isometric forms, the computer offers a greater range of options and consequently invites experimentation, particularly with perspective. This facility with perspective produces images that are closer to reality and therefore easier for non-professionals to understand. There is, however, a danger that the temptation to distort perspective to produce a more dramatic image may confuse rather than clarify. The purpose of every drawing is to convey information clearly and not to be an end in itself.

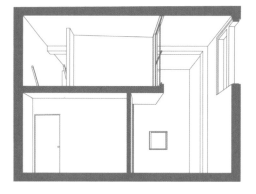

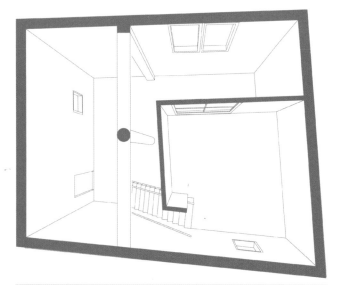

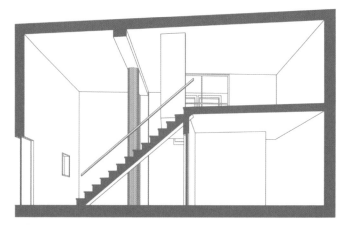

01
Plans may be projected upward in perspective, and this can make them more comprehensible. It is probably most effective for an interior on one level, in which all walls are visible.

02
With more than one floor level the conventional section, projected back in perspective, can sometimes explain the context of the section 'cut'.

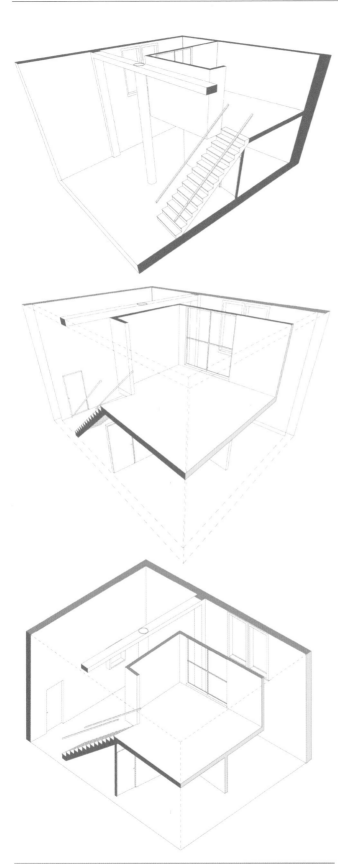

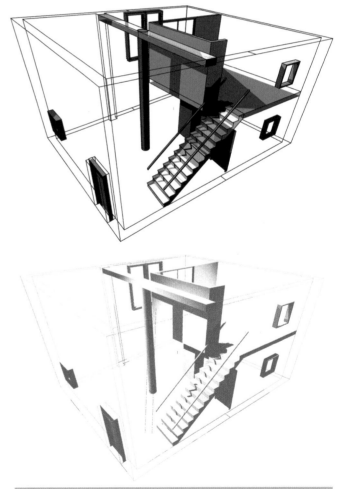

03
It is a matter of deciding which three-dimensional option works best for the project, and the computer allows options to be generated quickly and rotated on screen for consideration.

04
Further clarification of the three-dimensional may be achieved with the addition of tones and shadows, and the manner in which this is done again depends on the nature of the project. These two examples represent a few options.

Drawing by hand

Handmade drawings are normally made with either pen or pencil. The pen tends to be favoured when a more precise line is required, and this was particularly important in the days when dye-line printing was the most common method of reproducing drawings. The computer has now superseded the pen as the most effective means of making and reproducing precise drawings, in particular those providing technical information for building contractors. It is the more effective tool but, if drawings are any longer to be made by hand, it is perhaps logical that they should now be made in pencil because these have a quality that the computer cannot (yet) match.

The first sketches

The handmade drawing may have been superseded by the computer-generated image as the principle presentation tool but it retains its role as a first means of delineating and communicating ideas. To make such drawings does not require elaborate or sophisticated technique. In fact, too much reverence for the finished piece may result in time wasted in the refining of an image that has no value

Below
This pen drawing uses varying thicknesses of line, hatching and adhesive tone for additional articulation. Lines have the constant density of ink.

Below right
The pencil drawing has a richer patina. The plan and the construction lines used to set up the section and perspective have been retained, and the smudging that is inevitable in a complex pencil drawing contributes to the background texture. The weight applied to the pencil point provides variation in line quality and articulation of content.

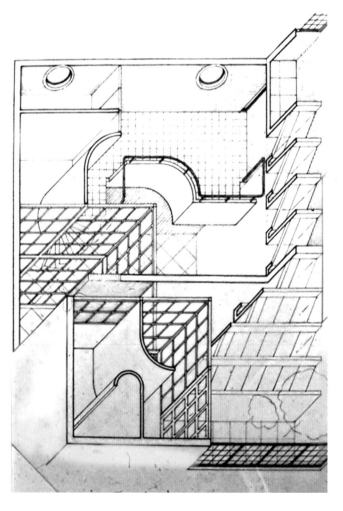

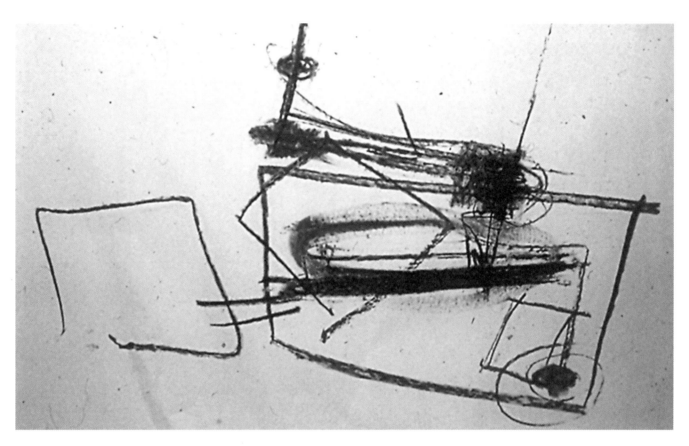

Left

This concise description of the curves that soften the lines of a stair is convincing because, although rudimentary, it has been made by someone who understands the mechanics of the stair, the proportional relationship of tread to riser and the essential structure. It does not solve the problems generated by those mechanics, but sets out aesthetic priorities.

Above

A very early, nearly abstract, exploratory drawing that holds meaning only for its maker.

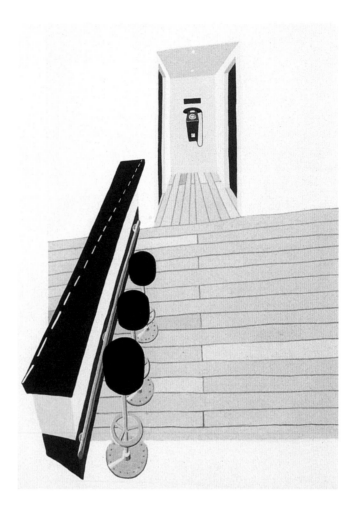

Above and top
The same internal elevation by day
and by night conveys information
effectively because it is simple and
precise.

Right
This very carefully composed
image pays enough attention to
perspective to be credible, but is
more concerned with the detail of
the simple elements that make up
the interior.

beyond the moment it delivers the information that is
revealed in its making. However – since designers tend, by
nature, to worry about the aesthetic merit of everything
they do – it is difficult not to tinker with a drawing once
it seems that it might have some merit in its own right,
even though the act of refining it can divert the mind
from consideration of its content. It is always difficult to
know exactly when a drawing is completed and has no
more insights to yield. Perhaps it is only when it appears
to be complete as an artefact that it becomes clear that
there is nothing to be gained from pursuing it further.

There is always a danger that if a drawing turns
out particularly well it may cloud judgement about the
quality of the idea it illustrates. It is difficult not to feel
some loyalty towards something that embodies style and
skill, but it is worth bearing in mind that any drawings
made in the development of a project are liable to, and
generally should, end in the waste-paper bin.

It is not surprising that it is difficult to find examples
of simple, utilitarian developmental drawings. Those
that are available are untypical, simply because they had
particular significance or because they were particularly
well made and their maker could not quite find the
resolve to throw them away.

The best way to make good drawings by hand is simply to make a lot of them, spontaneously, quickly, until it becomes something done almost without thinking. The intention is not to create a perfect set piece or a scrupulous observation of an existing object. There are no subtleties of light and shade to be captured. The thing to be drawn exists only in the imagination, and it is the serial act of trying to draw it that helps define its nature with ever increasing clarity.

The first drawings are likely to be crude, diagrammatic plans showing the subdivision of area and furniture layouts or simple perspective views with little indication of detail. These will become more detailed and precise as the design process progresses and as the designer gets increasingly clear insights into possibilities and limitations. It is important in every project that two- and three-dimensional drawings complement each other throughout development. The plans and sections allow the feasibility of the ideas expressed in the perspective views to be checked. Ultimately, the viability of any proposal depends on its relationship to the shell of the existing building in which it is to be located. In most cases the designer's ability to manipulate intricately the dimensions dictated by function in the context of the existing plan is key to success.

If a drawing is to be effective, its content should be credible but not necessarily precise. There are essential fundamentals and these should be aspired to and, if met, should ensure a convincing outcome.

Proportions and perspective should be accurate and plausible. Representation of light and shade should be kept simple, in order to define volumes with clarity. Wall tone will differ on either side of a corner because each will receive a different light, but the tone on each will be spread evenly – not in impressionistic textured blotches. The edges of shadows should be sharp and straight. Each drawing should have one consistent light source so that the convention used to articulate shapes is clear. If the play of light and shade becomes too complicated the point of the drawing is likely to be lost in an incoherence of graphic effects.

There are two ways to make a freehand perspective look convincing. The first is to render the perspective so 'wrong' that it may be assumed to be making no attempts to obey the rules – but this must be done with enough panache to confirm that it is deliberate. Alternatively, it should be near enough to being accurate to have credibility, and for this the proportions of the space drawn need to be accurate.

TIP HAND DRAWN LINES

Avoid 'hairy' artistic lines. Isolated and inadvertent line variation, as on the left, will appear as a drafting error. Controlled variation, as on the right, will absorb errors in a more deliberate 'freehand' effect. The concentration needed to control the variation will help keep the line straight.

It is important to be able to draw a convincing freehand approximation to a right angle. This is not difficult with some practice, and it easy to make a credible approximation to 45 and 30 degrees by subdivision of the 90. Where accuracy is particularly important, or where the shapes to be defined are complex, lines and angles may be drawn first, lightly and precisely, with technical instruments and then overdrawn freehand.

Accurate proportions can be guaranteed by accurate measurements, and a measured drawing does not have to be technically constructed. The same rules used to construct a technical drawing may be followed to make a freehand version, and a freehand line can be drawn to scale.

Making a simple freehand perspective

Establishing correct proportions is relatively easy. If the back wall of the space is drawn in elevation then, even when freehand, it can be measured for accurate proportions, as in the left-hand drawing, and the image established using the principles of single-point perspective, as in the right-hand drawing. For this, a vanishing point on the back wall must be established, usually off-centre and about 1600 millimetres (5 feet) above floor level for a standing view and 1100 millimetres (3½ feet) for a sitting view. However, any height is acceptable and the decision should be made on the basis of what will offer either the most informative or most persuasive view.

If lines are drawn from the vanishing point through the corners of the rectangle then the planes of the floor, walls and ceiling are established. The remaining decision is about how far they should project from the back wall. The most common mistake is to ignore the reality of foreshortening and project them too far. It is necessary to use judgement.

Once its boundaries have been established it is easy to make subdivisions within the space. Diagonals cross at the centre point of a plane. The rectangular areas thus created can be further subdivided by the same method and a line may be projected across the floor, from the vanishing point to these intersections, in order to

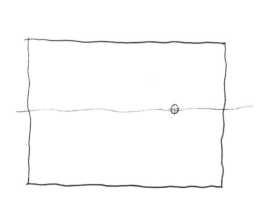

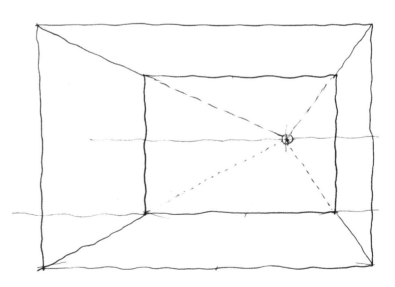

establish the position of the horizontal divisions in, for example, a tiled floor. The same principles may be applied to any of the planes. The position of an element may not precisely coincide with one of these divisions but can, again with intelligent judgement, be positioned plausibly.

The tendency will be to overestimate the length of side walls, and this may be acceptable when the perspective is distorted to allow clearer representation of elements within the space. There comes a point when it is preferable to move away from a credible perspective to something more diagrammatic. In 'true' perspective, elements tend to be superimposed one on the other and the information may be communicated more clearly if they are separated out. If the 'distortion' is handled positively, and clearly makes no attempt to create a true perspective, it will appear acceptable.

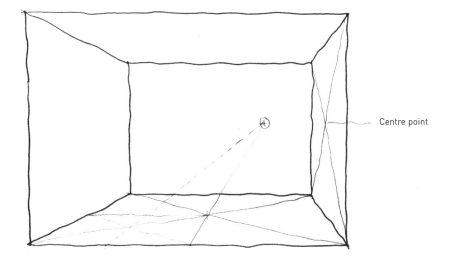

Centre point

This page and opposite
A sequence of drawings showing how a freehand perspective drawing is built up, beginning with the back wall and establishing a vanishing point (opposite left). In the next drawing (opposite right) walls and ceiling are added, and in the final drawing (left) the walls and ceilings are subdivided.

This page and opposite
Sequence of perspective drawings
in which the planes of the floor,
walls and other internal elements
are established using a vanishing
point and a viewpoint in front of
the plans.

Should it be desired, it is simple to establish the length of
side walls accurately:

The back wall is drawn to scale, with a vanishing
point as before, and a plan is drawn to the same scale and
in alignment. A viewpoint is established in front of the
plan. If it is too close, the side walls will appear too wide;
if too far away, they will be too narrow to reveal enough
detail.

The planes of floor, walls and ceiling are established
as before, but here the front edge of the space is
determined by lines drawn from the viewpoint to meet
the elongated line of the rear wall and projected vertically
upwards.

The same principles will convincingly set up volumes
within the space and may be applied to the location
of every element. However, there will come a point
when there is no need for this degree of precision and
further drawing may be made relative to the reference
points provided by the first plotted locations. In fact,
it is probably undesirable if too much deliberation is
employed because the drawing will lose the charm of the
freehand sketch.

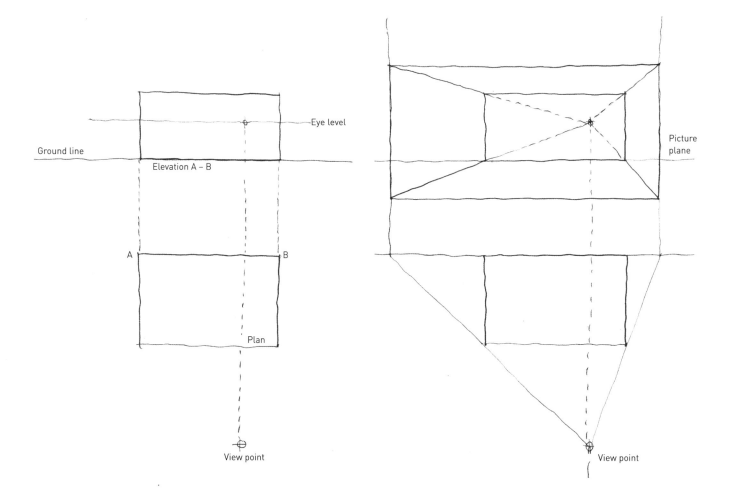

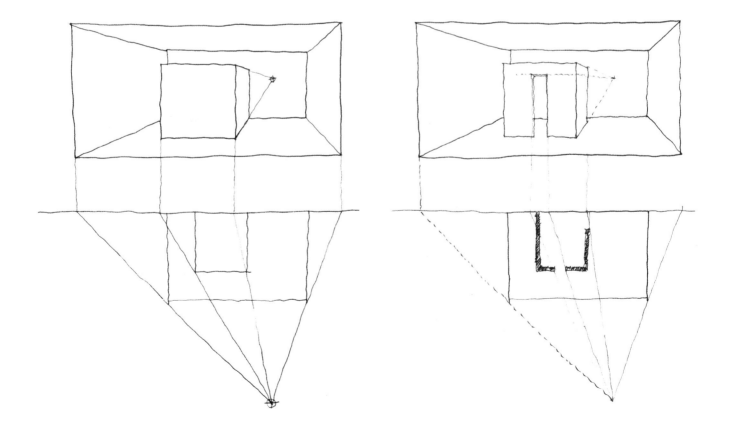

Axonometric and isometric projections

Freehand perspectives are difficult to set up because lines converge towards shared vanishing points. An axonometric or isometric drawing, which relies on parallel lines, avoids this and is extremely easy to draw with or without instruments.

The principles for constructing these types of view are simple. Plans are drawn at angles, the axonometric at 45 degrees to the horizontal, as a true plan. An isometric is made with the two walls nearest to the viewer at 30 degrees to the horizontal, which results in distortion of the plan but opens the spaces up more in the final drawing. In both projections, vertical lines are drawn to the same scale as the plan. While neither method creates a true perspective, both give a convincing sense of three dimensions. The results may be treated as diagrams or rendered to give a more realistic impression of finishes and lighting. The axonometric is easier to draw by hand. The computer deals equally easily with both.

When making an axonometric it is crucial to concentrate on establishing one corner that conforms credibly to the basic principles, that the front corner be drawn at 45 degrees to the horizontal. The plan and elevations are not distorted and so it is important to

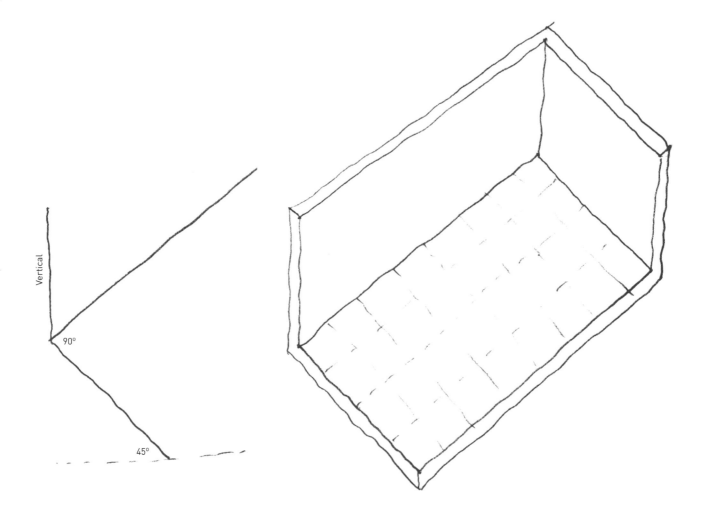

create a right angle on the corner and to draw the edge
of the wall precisely vertically. After those few lines are
established, it is easy to follow the rules to complete
the whole. It is not difficult to judge angles and relative
dimensions by eye if one concentrates and critically
assesses the drawing as it takes shape. If an area is
unsatisfactory it is easy to retrace over the flawed original
and correct its shortcomings.

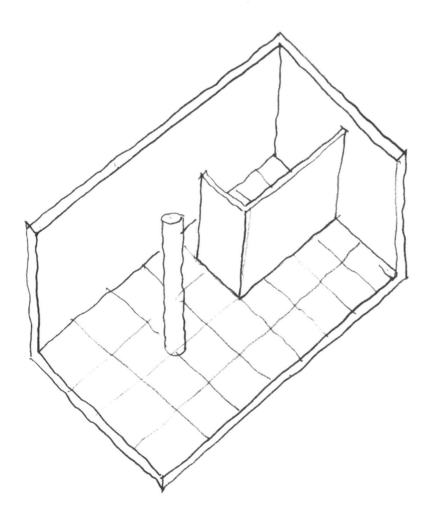

This page and opposite
This example is a tracing of the
basic form of an axonometric
drawing made with technical
instruments, a scale ruler and a
set square. The advantage of a
freehand tracing of a constructed
base drawing is that it can be
done much faster than a wholly
technical construction and does
not require the same detailed
level of finish. It is important,
in fact, that a tracing is not too
conscientious or the drawing will
lose its dynamic.

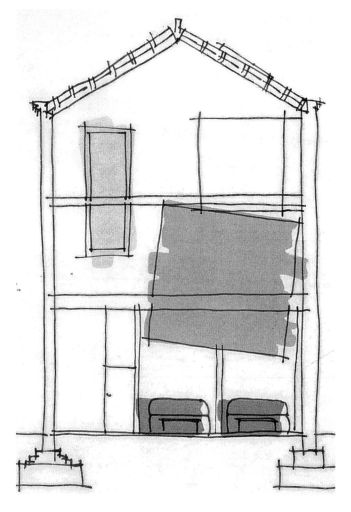

Overlays

For overlays, tracing paper offers complete transparency. Detailing paper, which is thin and white, offers something which is less transparent, but through which the dark lines of an underlay will show. The semi-transparency of detail paper makes it easier to add colour to it. Choice of material is, as always, a personal matter, but to reject a degree of transparency in favour of the more familiar texture of cartridge or another wholly opaque paper necessitates making a fresh, scaled drawing of the existing building shell for each new drawing.

When making design drawings by hand, a tracing of the existing building shell is particularly useful. Traced freehand drawings will be accurate enough, and significant measurements such as the dimensions of rooms, width of doors or size of furniture can be made with a scale rule. Such elements, which in turn have a broadly standardized and recognizable size, give insight into the reality and feasibility of the proposed spaces. If measurements are not checked, there is a counter-productive tendency to be optimistic about sizes and lose track of the realities of restricted spaces.

Frequently, when an early proposal requires rethinking, the rejected scaled drawing can be used as the underlay for a return to freehand sketching. Successive drawings can be made quickly, and thinking once again expressed with a spontaneity that allows new ideas to flow and build momentum. The slower pace of making accurate mechanical drawings makes time for attention and the imagination to wander.

Whether considering a project for the first time

TIP DIMENSIONS IN FREEHAND DRAWINGS

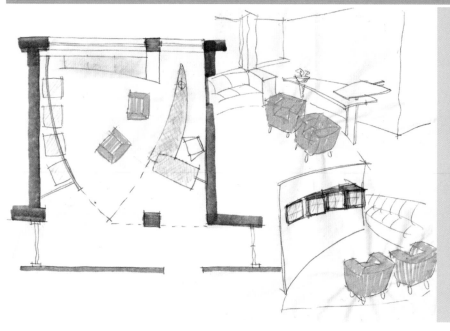

A facility for mental arithmetic is useful when making freehand drawings. When the dimensions of rooms and wall thicknesses are known it is reassuring to check practicalities, such as circulation spaces, mathematically, even though the drawing itself may not be precise. A working knowledge of standard furniture dimensions provides useful visual indicators of relative scale. In this example circulation around and behind the curved desk looks restricted and suggests that the seat below the window must be adjusted to create space.

or trying to reorientate thinking to solve a newly
apparent problem, there is some virtue in repeatedly
redrawing wall thicknesses and the locations of
windows and doors because each reiteration reinforces
awareness of the nature of the existing building. An
interior contained within thick stone walls will suggest
different interventions from one within less substantial
construction. Similarly, it is good practice to trace the
features of the existing shell for each new freehand
drawing in order to build the same awareness of context.
The traced freehand version will inevitably be faster,
and a scaled grid of graph paper offers an alternative
measuring system.

Opposite
A quickly traced section, in which
crucial old and new elements are
identified by coloured felt tips.

Above
This very ordered internal elevation
may have been prompted by the
decision to draw on graph paper
– or may have influenced the same
decision after the nature of the
solution had emerged. Whatever
the sequence, the grid made the
location and sizing of elements
simpler.

Freehand drawing for presentation

Freehand drawings can be useful for initial presentations, particularly during early discussions when it is more important to get insight into a client's preferences than to secure definitive approvals. They provide a quick way to make drawings when discussion suddenly becomes important – or when it is necessary to demonstrate effort and some progress.

It is, however, seldom a good idea to confront a client with a collection of crude diagrams on scraps of paper, and it is unlikely that any preliminary sketches will stand scrutiny as serious presentation material. The inevitable weaker sections will undermine strong areas of drawing. By contrast, the computer may be slower but it tends to guarantee an acceptable outcome.

While more polished versions of early drawings are preferable for presentation purposes, it is also desirable that the final version retains some of the flourishes and energy of the developmental sketches. Unsatisfactory freehand passages, typically deficiencies in perspective and proportion, may be corrected by tracing over the whole and eliminating weaknesses. Areas that work

Above

These apparently simple drawings nevertheless convince because they are made vigorously – and the perspective is credible. The delineation of the seating makes it obvious that the designer has specific examples in mind. The representation of the glass table's transparency is particularly effective. The suggestion of panel joints on the curved form indicates that thinking is being shaped by an awareness of construction.

Right

A few of the pencil lines that initially set up this gouache sketch remain visible, but most are lost under the vigorously applied paint. The concern is more with describing atmosphere than detail, which is only hinted at in representations of furniture. The energy of the image was enough to persuade a sceptical client to commit to the project.

may be retained. However, to sustain the vigour of the drawing it is a good idea to retrace all the lines quickly to avoid making an image that appears to aspire to precision and might therefore have been made more effectively with technical instruments.

The photocopier and the computer scanner also allow the size of an image to be adjusted. Changes in size frequently seem to improve the quality of the original, and this can also be a useful way to suggest that a number of disparate sketches, when printed to a similar size, comprise a set. A reduction in size gives a density of drawing that may be missing in the original, and inflating the size develops textures of line, particularly when the original is made with a soft pencil, that will not necessarily be apparent in the original.

It is not usually good practice to draw large in the first instance. A large drawing will generally invite or require more detail and inevitably take, and therefore waste, more time. Credible perspective in particular is much more difficult to sustain in a large drawing and requires more care to make. It is more physically comfortable to draw at a small scale, perhaps within the confines of an A5 page, but individual preference should determine sizes and media.

There is one category of drawing at which the hand excels, and that is the diagram. Interior design projects are very frequently complex and it is good practice to introduce clients to them in a series of steps, which make the salient points clearly and sequentially. These can be made using computer-generated views, but a computer image tends to be less effective when it is too simple. Like any other tool it is most effective when its strengths are exploited, and the computer's strength is the generation of complex form and subtle rendering. Complex images do not necessarily make good diagrams. The handmade diagram that deals only with a single, crucial idea can exactly explain principles and intentions.

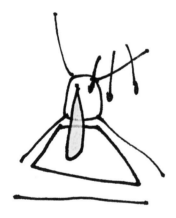

Above
An elemental diagram suggesting the planes of a room, hanging lights and perhaps a figure.

Right
Traced plans, in which problem areas are identified on the left by the hatched lines, and the proposed solution shown in red on the right.

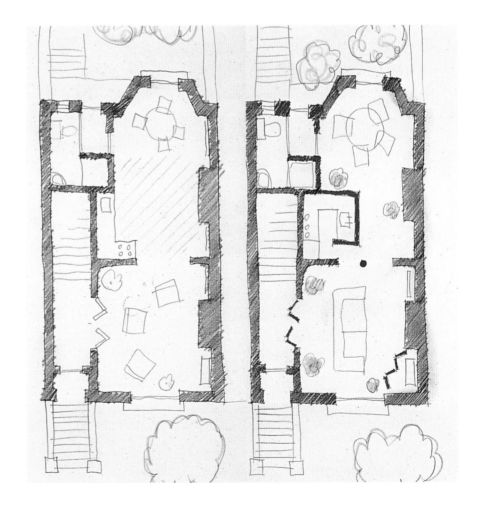

Below left
The wooden pencil remains viable but needs constant sharpening. More sophisticated, mechanical pencils offer consistent line width. Some, like that on the bottom, provide a thick heavy line for sketching. Others, like that on the top, offer precisely controlled line width and a choice of lead types.

Bottom left
Pens like that on the bottom use cartridges of dense, usually black, drawing ink and offer a choice of exact line thicknesses, which are useful in the articulation of drawing content. The thinnest nibs (0.1 and 0.13 mm) are vulnerable and expensive. Felt-tipped pens, like that on the top, come in a variety of line thicknesses but do not offer the same degree of precision, and, although cheaper, do not last long.

Bottom right
Compasses make circles or set up angles (see page 28). They can be adapted, as on the right, to take mechanical pencils and drawing pens.

Hand-drawing tools

While there is no doubt that the computer has become the tool of choice and a necessity for large and small practices, there is no reason why hand drawing should not survive as an alternative, perhaps most viable for the slightly eccentric individual practitioner working on small-scale projects.

Freehand sketching provides an effective and immediate way to visualize concepts in the earliest stages of the design process, but to develop ideas it quickly becomes essential to work accurately to scale, to understand how plans and sections should be organized and to refine the interaction and relative proportions of new and existing elements. The tools and instruments illustrated on these pages, together with a drawing board with a T-square or parallel motion arm, ensure the necessary level of accuracy.

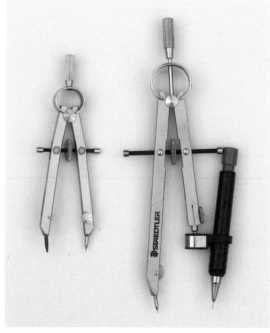

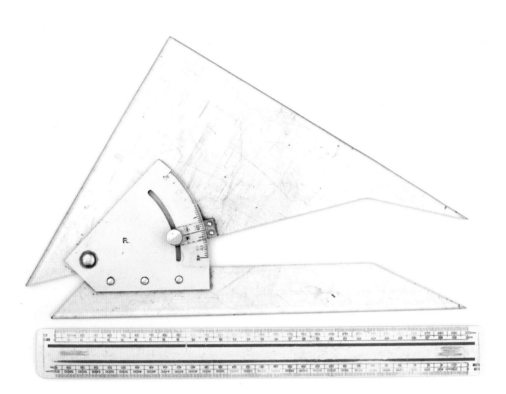

Left

Rulers have the necessary range of standard drawing scales arranged over both faces. An adjustable set square, combined with a T-square or parallel motion arm on a drawing board, creates accurate angles.

Below

Circle templates come with a comprehensive range of radii options and 'French curves' define more complex shapes. Stencils, for both pen and pencil, make clear lettering but are time-consuming and can discourage neat note writing.

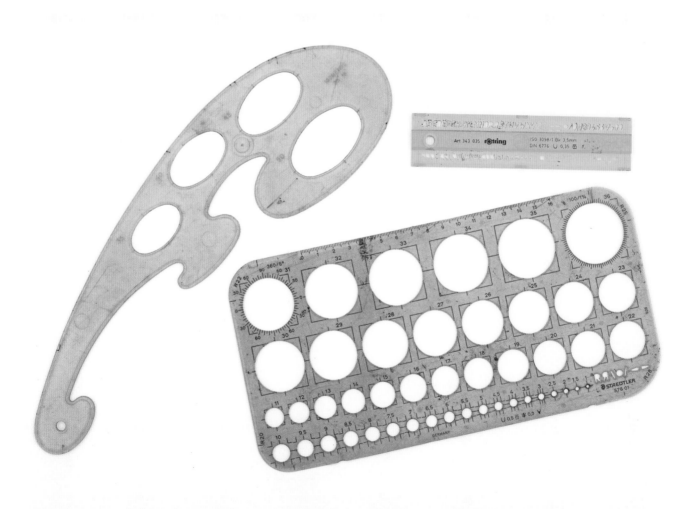

A handmade presentation sequence

Often the significant development of projects is initiated and resolved through handmade drawings. While the transition to computer for final presentation and production drawing is now almost inevitable, the point at which the transition is made depends largely on personal preference. In this example the designer, trained in conventional techniques and with a particularly strong drafting style, chose to exploit those strengths in making drawings for an initial client presentation.

To develop the idea the designer had to work much more accurately to understand the potential, and limitations, of the existing building, in particular the problem of how to relate the new multi-levelled structure to the vaulted ceiling and rooflight within it. While a plan will determine the size of rooms and the circulation between them, it is the section that most effectively explores the potential of the dramatic volume – and identifies the peripheral spaces where the more utilitarian activities such as bathrooms and storage may be accommodated. The brown tissue paper fixed to the reverse side of the transparent tracing paper, which quite accurately represents the exposed pink plaster finish, also identifies the perimeters of one dwelling unit within the whole. Shading indicates how light from the window in the sloping external roof filters down to the horizontal internal window and through it to the living spaces below. Chairs help establish scale.

It is common practice to draw all or parts of a project to increasingly larger scales, to allow closer scrutiny of aspects of the design and to identify the areas where thought must be given to construction techniques. Often, as in this case, there will be few substantial changes, but drawing to a larger scale can point to areas that are potentially awkward to resolve visually and to allow speculation about smaller scale detail. In the example on the left, opposite, the fixing of the handrail and the way it ends against its supporting wall is a small but vital progression. There is also some further thought about the proportions and framing of door openings. Even if such larger scale drawing were not to result in any changes, which are unlikely, drawing and re-drawing would still be an important part of the design process because the repetitive act obliges a designer to reflect critically on ideas evolved at the smaller scale.

While designers working on a project may understand very clearly the three-dimensional implications of their own plans and sections, it is less apparent to clients, and frequently to other designers. It therefore makes sense to produce freehand three-dimensional sketches that clarify the interrelationships. It is important to make sure, particularly in a domestic project, that clients understand exactly what is being discussed and its implications, if they are to make an effective contribution to the development of the whole. As shown in the first diagram in this sequence,

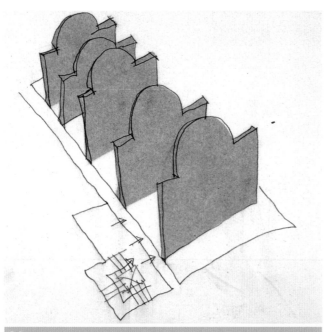

01
Information is edited to the minimum to concentrate attention on the essential subdivision of the existing building shell. Dimensional accuracy is not as important as clarity of communication.

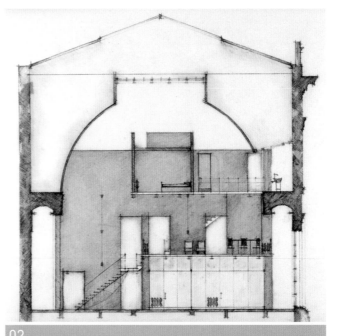

02
The precise relationship between the new and existing elements can only be effectively established with a drawing made to scale. Traditional instruments will produce an acceptable level of accurate detail.

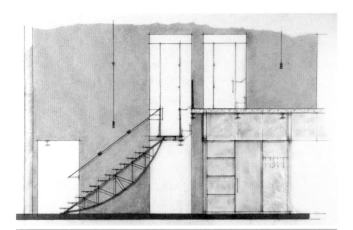

03
This larger, scaled area of the elevation allows more detailed examination of the smaller elements: light fittings, handrail fixings, even door handles.

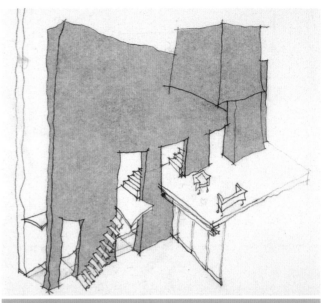

04
Another three-dimensional diagrammatic sketch helps clarify the relationship of the three levels and the stairs that connect them. It is again simplified for clarity.

simplification of the image is important for clarity. Non-essentials such as handrails and light fittings are omitted.

It should also be acknowledged that making such drawings has a productive therapeutic effect on the designer. They offer a brief relief from making the detailed technical images that demand the simultaneous consideration and reconciliation of aesthetic and practical priorities, and a more disciplined and intense drawing technique. They may also occasionally identify potential physical clashes between elements that were previously unsuspected in two dimensions. Most designers will quickly scribble three-dimensional views, for their own enlightenment, in the course of making plans and sections. These may, occasionally, be upgraded for presentation purposes. This habitual introspective scribbling is a useful way of maintaining a freehand drawing skill that can be useful when it becomes necessary to produce spontaneously an explanatory sketch in response to a client's question. Such ad hoc drawing may be the last hand drawing activity to be superseded by the computer and, if it is done well, it will always impress a client – or colleague.

Presentation sheets

Presentation sheets are usually composites of a number of different drawings and, particularly with freehand drawing, it is difficult to place individual drawings together on a single sheet and next to impossible to sustain a compatible quality across the group. It is seldom satisfactory to present scraps of tracing paper to a client, and mounting them on card is a rather grandiose way to present modest scribbles. It is better to photocopy them and to present them singly as, say, A4 sheets. This retains an appropriate informality. If it is considered worth presenting a number together, for example to make a sequential explanation, individual drawings may be arranged and copied on to a single sheet. Computer scanning is superior to photocopying in that it reproduces accurately the quality of line and medium.

Collage

The majority of interior projects do not require elaborate manipulation of floor levels and walls, and while those that do may be superficially more spectacular, they are not necessarily more successful than those relying on the comparatively modest devices of carefully selected materials, colours and lighting effects. All these are notoriously difficult and time-consuming to represent by hand, and collage offers an alternative to the computer early in the design process. Those who favour the technique build a stock of colours and textures, usually clipped from magazines and identified as reliable sources. Such images, roughly pasted together, can take on some of the characteristics and authority of the well-crafted object, and source materials are scanned by computer and manipulated to take greater account of perspective and scale. With their deliberate lack of dimensional and

Right and far right
While a line drawing defines planes, it does not easily convey three-dimensional form. Collaged papers in different colours and tones, roughly cut to the shape of the proposed element, give a sense of solidity. The monochromatic version on the far right, created on computer, concentrates on form.

TIP COLOURED TISSUE

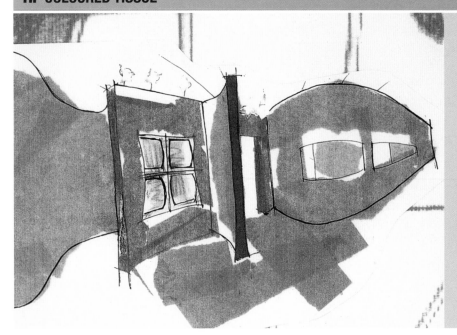

It is always difficult to represent flat masses of colour in any drawing. Here, tissue papers provide the blocks of colour that indicate different wall and floor finishes. The tissues are applied to the back of the tracing paper, which filters the intensity of their colours. They are cut or torn roughly to shape and lightly sprayed with fixative in order to position them permanently enough to survive the copying process. Since they have a degree of transparency it is possible, once they are fixed, to cut them with a scalpel to match exactly the outlines of planes.

Left

In this drawing on tracing paper, a black ink line roughly defines the space. The collaged photographs of pink stools give credibility to the more roughly presented elements. The sketched stools are finished with coloured pencils on the front of the tracing paper, which avoids damaging the tissue papers that provide colour for the walls and floor.

Below

A quick line drawing on tracing paper is given solidity by the collaged blocks of textured colour. The freehand drawing works particularly well because of the convincing perspective of both sets of curved steps.

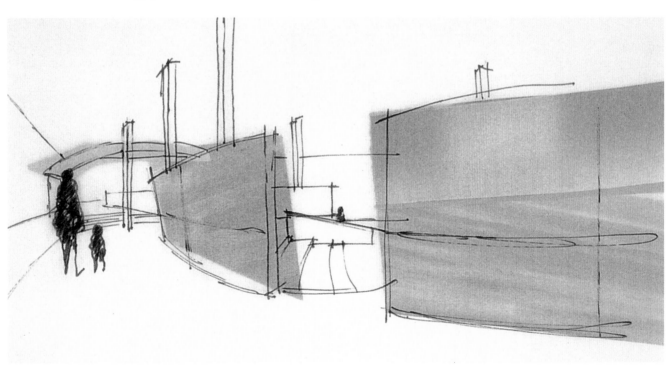

perspectival precision, these images will, and should, make clear that they intend to offer only an impression of the proposed interior.

Obviously, in collage-work the representation of colours is dictated by the limited range of papers and images available. However, if a handmade drawing is scanned on computer, then blocks of colour and texture may be matched accurately and further refinements – like representation of transparency, reflectivity and light – may also be added. Increasingly, it makes sense to resort to the computer, which copies and pastes more efficiently.

Collages, once cut and pasted, can be improved if photocopied to make a flat, integrated image. Digital scanning offers superior copying quality and the image created can be manipulated further on the computer.

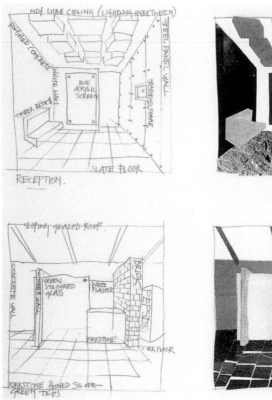

Above
A photocopy of crumpled white paper provides a complex random pattern that suggests marble.

Above right
While precision in a collage may be difficult, ambiguities can be avoided if the collaged image is paired with a line drawing that provides a key to the materials proposed.

Left
A traditional cut-and-pasted collage was scanned and the colour tones were adjusted in the computer to get closer to the designer's intentions.

Right
This image uses the principles of collage but was achieved solely with scanner and computer. The green and grey receding planes were created purely as a computer image, but the yellow-and-black image on the left and the column on the right were scanned and pasted. The figures were downloaded from an image website and pasted – or collaged – in, but adjusted for varying degrees of transparency.

1.56LOW RES

1:50

Technical drawings made by hand, particularly using a pencil, are comparable in accuracy to those made on a computer but they have a very different patina. Hand drawn lines are softer and will be slightly blurred by the passage of the T-squares and set squares across them as the drawing progresses. In the example on the left the effect achieved is with pastel dust rubbed into the reverse side of tracing paper using a soft cloth or tissue paper so that the defining line is not obscured. Colours and tone are varied in intensity to suggest changing light and textures. Denser colours are made with coloured pencils, crosshatched and rubbed with a finger to eliminate directional lines. The finished product has character but is a one-off and, unlike a computer-made alternative, cannot be adapted or easily amended.

Some adjustment and development is possible, however. Working with tracing paper allows drawings to be built up in layers and individual elements to be combined for a more complex presentation. In the composite drawing on the right, a strip of blue paper, first fixed to a white base sheet, represents the sea and highlights the contour of the coastal site, represented by a fragment of map. The tracing paper with the red-walled building, drawn to one side, is fixed over the other layers. The whole may be shown within a transparent sleeve or photocopied to produce a single sheet. There will be some blurring – of the bottom image in particular – but if this is not conveying detailed information, the distortion is acceptable.

Above
Hand drawn sketches, such as this section, allow a certain amount of graphic spontaneity and flamboyance.

Opposite
In this composite drawing a plan is drawn on tracing paper. Underneath this layer red tissue paper has been placed to indicate solid walls, and a location plan with blue paper to indicate water.

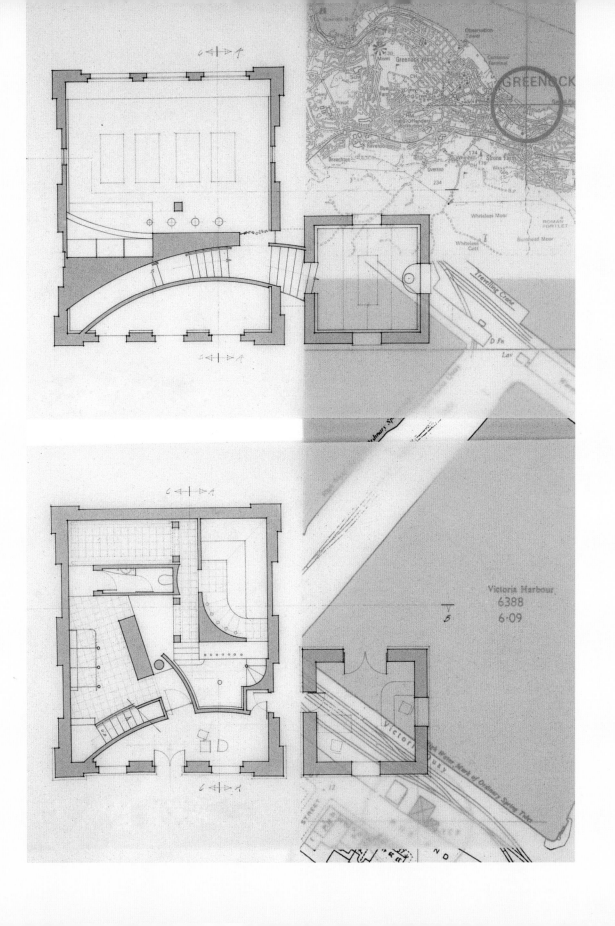

Chapter 2
Conception

Exploratory drawings

Every project begins with an idea that has to be defined and refined. A first idea that is little more than an informed presumption, made with limited understanding of either the precise requirements of the brief or the quirks of the building shell within which it must be interpreted, is unlikely to survive intact to the end of the development process. The more ambitious the concept, the more difficult it is likely to be to resolve – and the more time that resolution is likely to require.

The first drawings may be no more than thoughts about a strategy for organizing a space to accommodate a new function: a suggestion of where new walls might be located, for example, or how furniture could be arranged. Alternatively, they might attempt to describe an atmosphere, although that could be done just as effectively in words or in a collage of found images. First drawings should, in fact, be whatever they have to be to do their job: to record ideas, to examine them and to communicate them to others. They are likely to be very simple, perhaps no more than diagrams. They may

well be – and perhaps are liable to be – quick, handmade scribbles, although, as computer software becomes easier and quicker to use and as designers emerge who are more adept at employing it, the earliest images may increasingly emerge from the computer.

Such exploratory drawings tend to be idiosyncratic because they are for the designer's own information and are made without too much concern for their aesthetic merit. Nevertheless, they provide the reference point that will orientate and reorientate thinking throughout detailed development, and are therefore particularly important when a team of designers is collaborating on a project. Most members of such a team will not be involved in the project's conception, and all will have not only different responsibilities but also different degrees of responsibility within the development process, and will need to understand and share a common objective – and that can be encapsulated in these early drawings.

While the first drawing may be the significant reference point, the intention it represents will develop

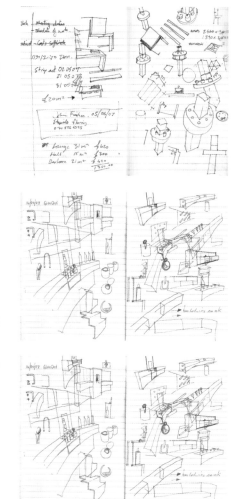

Left
A very early sketch, made with coloured felt-tip pens in a lined notepad, captured the essence of an idea to be refined and tuned to the specifics of the brief. The 'foot' motif is obviously the starting point and subsequent detail – the shape of the light fittings and foreground chairs – is sympathetic to it. Other elements – the curve on the ceiling, the parallel lines on the floor – indicate that ideas about finishes are evolving. The recess that contains the desk, the suspended ceiling element and the projecting wall beside the door indicate an awareness of the physical realities of the space.

Right
Pages from a notebook illustrate how ideas persist and are explored throughout the design process. Some of the forms that dominate the middle pages are beginning to emerge in another project in the right-hand book.

as understanding of the project evolves. In fact, however clear and powerful a first idea may appear to be it ought to evolve. The longer one works on a project the more closely one becomes aware of the complexities of the interaction between the brief requirements and the realities of the existing building shell. The early conceptual diagram will inevitably change. In fact, it should be a matter of concern if no changes suggest themselves. They may prove to be unnecessary, but there is inevitably a danger of complacency or, as is more often the case, a stubborn commitment to sustaining a seductive first idea at the expense of practical priorities.

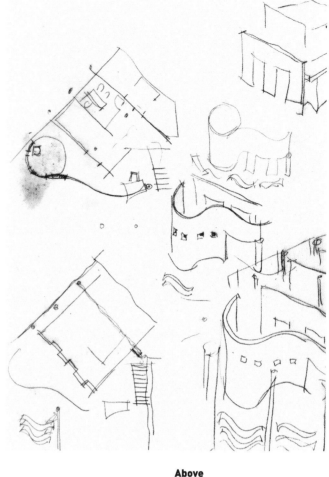

Above
The ground- and first-floor plans on the left of the page were made as overlays on the plan of an existing building, but the only evidence of this is in the circular representations of columns that determine the practical location for new walls. The sketches on the right speculate about the extrusion of the plan, showing options for the curved wall and heights of walls and balustrades. They are drawn from above to emphasize the relationship between plans and elevations.

Left
This sketchbook drawing records early speculation about how new elements might interact with the existing building. A scribbled note explains how the stair will be excavated from the existing concrete floor, and the drawing makes clear that the rough-hewn concrete treads will be supported on a delicate structure and that the 'excavation' will remain exposed.

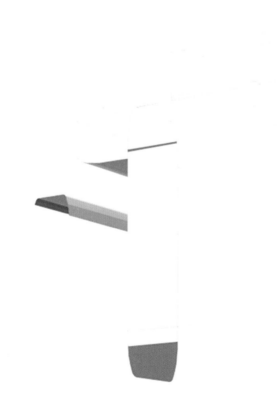

Left

Another quick sketch, made with pastels on white paper, showing clear thinking about how the elements – steps, small recesses and spotlights – will work together. Colour used in the drawing is determined by available pastels, so can only suggest the final hue.

Below

Another computer-generated image that deals diagrammatically, but accurately, with form. The figures give a sense of scale.

Below
This computer-generated image remains quite abstract, and was made in order to distil the designer's ideas about form and materials but not intended to communicate very much to anyone else.

The plan

A designer will begin the development of a concept by sketching out and refining the plan. The following pair of sheets from an A4 tracing block give some idea of the progression of thoughts and the drawings which prompt and record them.

Dimensions and proportions

Even when making the most rudimentary first sketches, the dimensions and proportions of the building shell must be acknowledged. The difficulty of making the first drawings is that no tangible model exists for replication or interpretation. The proposal exists only in the designer's imagination and it is easy for things to become unrealistic and for impossible ambitions to take over. Informed awareness of the realities of the existing space can structure thoughts about new elements. Almost all interior-design projects require the insertion of the maximum possible accommodation into a space that was originally designed to contain some other function, and unstructured drawing can encourage counterproductive optimism. A solution carelessly conceived for an imagined long, low space will fail in the reality of a tall, narrow one.

Getting the proportions of freehand sketches, whether two or three dimensional, correct requires no more than self-critical concentration. Freehand drawings may be used late in the design process if they are (roughly) scaled, and existing elements located (fairly)

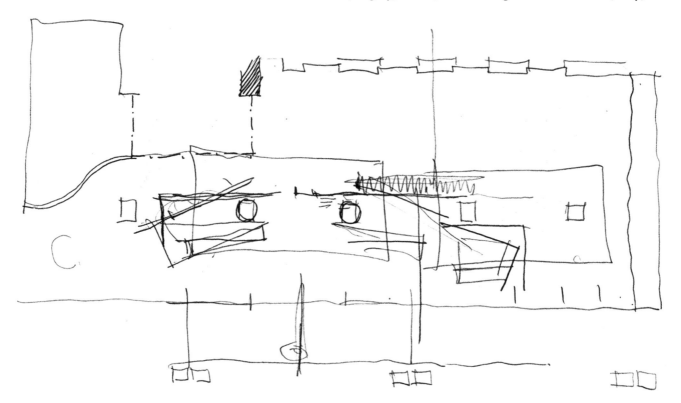

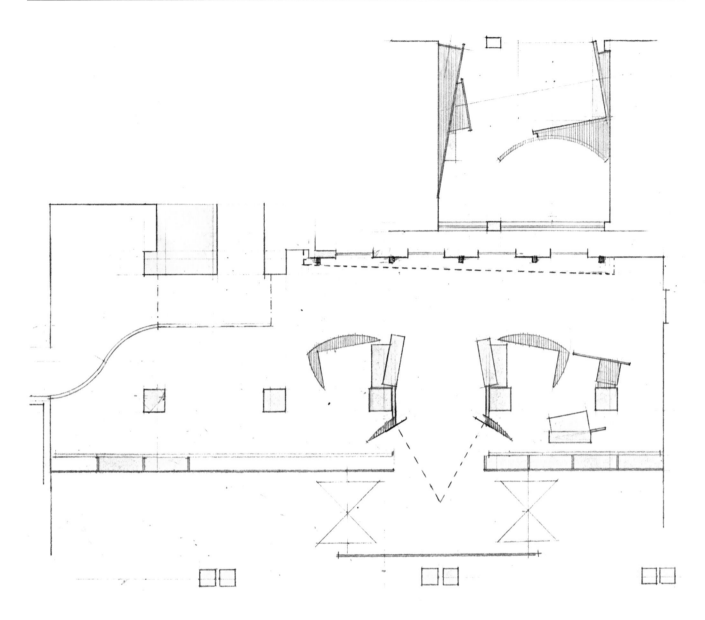

accurately will provide constant reference points for the positioning of new features.

The earliest sketches are likely to be three-dimensional images, but once a strategy has been defined its development must be resolved in the two dimensions of plan and section. Ideas about form, materiality and atmosphere need to be precisely plotted, and it is sensible to make these drawings to scale.

The mind needs to be focused on the job of designing and it is productive to allow momentum to build, so that each drawing follows the other with a minimum of interruption – no longer than it takes to place the accurate base drawing below another sheet of transparent paper – so that thoughts flow effortlessly to and from each other. There are moments, however, when the 'tempo' of drawing can, and should, vary. When an idea is being hotly pursued, one drawing will flow spontaneously from the other with only the most minimal delineation of new elements being superimposed

on the lines of the existing plan that show through a transparent overlay. However, sometimes it is important to slow the tempo in order to marshal thoughts. Then it may be productive to draw the existing plan or section again, but precisely, to refocus attention on its particularities, its wall thicknesses, its window sizes and door positions – and to test the relationship of the new elements to the old.

The internal elevation

A selection of drawings made with pencil, pastel and coloured pencil on tracing paper, show the development of the internal elevations for a cinema project.

Drawings, however perfunctory, record the decisions made in the progression of a project. They enable retrospective analysis to be made, in order to identify what is working and to provide material for an examination of where momentum or direction was lost.

While the ambiguity of the freehand drawing leaves room for creative interpretation, the precision of computer-generated images can also prompt fresh thinking. The hard facts of the first tentative plans and sections may be converted spontaneously into rudimentary three-dimensional expressions of the anticipated space, and these, in turn, may be explored further by rotating them in the virtual space of the monitor screen. Unanticipated possibilities may be glimpsed in the previously unexplored detail of the proposal, whereas the handmade drawing can only offer a version of what is already anticipated and understood in the designer's imagination.

01
Two- and three-dimensional consideration of how internal walls might elevate, and how areas might be physically and visually connected.

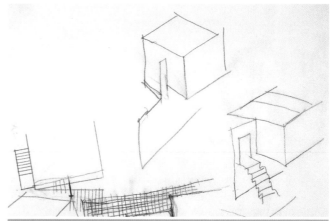

02
A fragment of a larger drawing focuses on resolving the intersections of secondary elements.

03
The first (roughly) measured elevation of an internal wall. Ancillary or, as yet, unresolved elements are drawn freehand and figures are added for scale.

04
Shadows begin to suggest the effect of lighting, and this is examined in much greater detail in this final, rendered, scaled drawing. Ideas about lighting and materials are beginning to crystallize.

The first presentations

Clients tend to be suspicious of proposals presented to them. They have a lot to lose financially and an poor interior condemns them to extended existence in an uncongenial environment. Their views should be solicited early and often, they need to be given enough evidence to make an informed contribution to the development of the project and there is something about a meeting with even the most amiable client that makes a designer's adrenalin pump and new ideas flow. It is counterproductive in the long term to persuade clients, with seductively inaccurate images, to accept a proposal that ignores their wishes and their needs. Drawings should be easily understood, and it helps if they can meet the client's expectations of what a drawing should look like. Some will welcome evidence of artistic flair, and so may appreciate expressionistic or impressionistic images. Others will be reassured by something that may appear to be more technically orientated. All will expect evidence of practical and technical efficiency. However, the drawings, like the project itself, should give them not only what they expected but something additional and desirable that they were not anticipating.

Design sketches

It is important to consider how 'finished' drawings should look in early discussions. If something definitive is presented for discussion before its practical feasibility has been resolved, there is a danger that the client will be seduced by an impossible proposal and expect to see it built. Something less definitive, just enough to structure a productive conversation, is safe and more productive because it will encourage conversation that will enhance both sides' understanding of the brief.

Developing the concept

The most complex projects begin with an idea, usually no more than an intuitive hunch. Most designers will make their first records and investigations of this starting point in quick freehand sketches in which they can begin to glimpse the physical shape that their untested proposition may take. As they sketch they also begin to understand better not only what they should do but what they can do. A good designer does not force an inappropriate concept but rather identifies how the requirements of the brief and the nature of the existing building can be reconciled. This understanding can only be properly achieved when details of both are dealt with precisely and, inevitably this requires more controlled, scaled drawings, using conventions that allow the interaction of new and existing elements to be accurately plotted in two dimensions. While these may deal with prosaic practicalities, they also allow aesthetic fine-tuning of proportion. They may be made traditionally by hand on a drawing board, or, as is now the norm, on computer, which also eases the conversion of data accumulated in plan and section to a rendered three-dimensional form. Every successful interior evolves in this search for a satisfactory balance of intuition and objectivity.

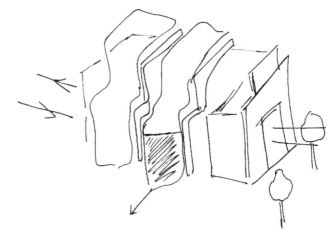

01
A freehand diagram explaining a possible design strategy.

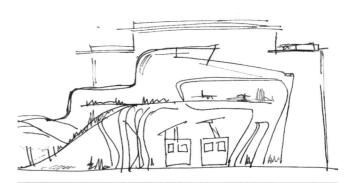

02
A more careful consideration of how new elements linking the interior to the exterior might relate to the existing building (not yet drawn to scale).

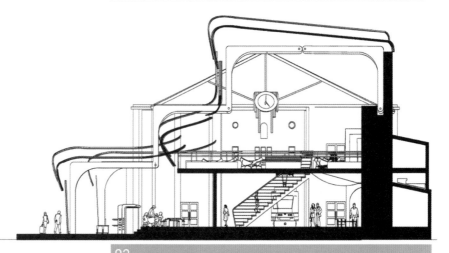

03
When the ideas are transferred to computer and the new elements, the existing building and site boundaries are drawn accurately, the configuration changes significantly — and for the better.

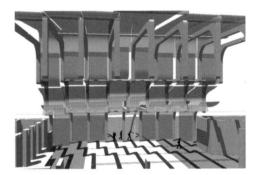

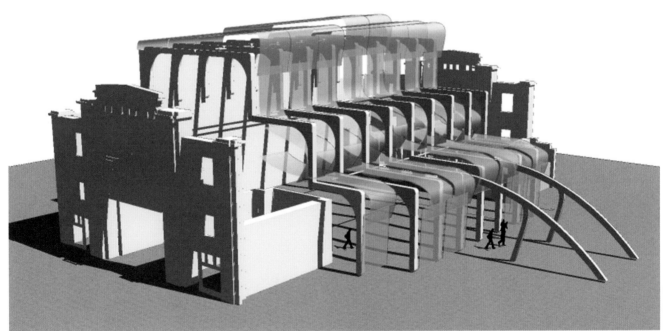

04

The new forms and their relationship to the existing building are comprehensively described in the final, comparatively diagrammatic, sketches.

A diagrammatic sketch, prepared for a preliminary client meeting introduces a strategy for circulation through a shopping mall.

The simplicity and clarity of the diagram recognize that participants in the meeting will not necessarily be comfortable with more complex technical drawings, particularly if these are exclusively two-dimensional. A simple diagram helps understanding of the crucial ideas under consideration, and ensures that everyone can contribute confidently to the discussion. The view from above explains how the plan translates into three dimensions.

All the elements in the image are reduced to essentials. Colour is added to the 'navigational banners', making them dominant. The lift shaft and stairs are confidently delineated, but visually reduced to a minimum and relegated to the background. Casually sketched but unmistakable 'customers' give scale, and those at the upper level explain how floors interact. Written notes are kept to an essential minimum – just enough to act as aides-mémoires during discussions, stating facts but not insinuating aesthetic values.

The informality of the drawing suggests that the project remains at a formative stage, still open for discussion. The cartoonish quality encourages relaxed, productive conversation, but the accomplished and confident handling of line and perspective lends the proposal credibility and its designer the authority to lead the meeting.

This sketch provides another layer of information about elements in the previous drawing. It retains a degree of ambiguity, leaving scope for negotiation without committing the designer to specific outcomes before principles have been examined and options comprehensively discussed. Stylized figures again suggest scale and explain how the space will be used: the figure with the pram leaving the lift gives reassurance that practicalities have not been neglected.

Greater attention to detail is signalled by the indication of floor and ceiling patterns, and the joints of cladding panels on the lift shaft. Some of this drawing, such as the implication of lights on the front of the lift shaft, is in all likelihood spontaneous speculation made as the drawing

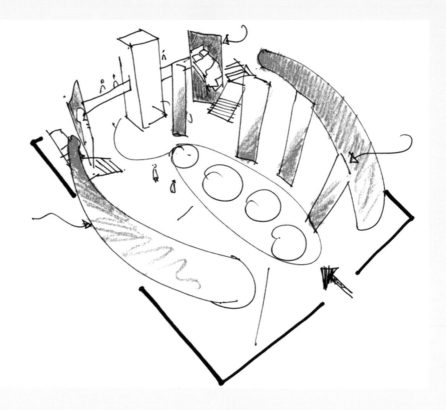

is produced, but is enough to suggest that there is unexplored potential. The precise location of lights, on and halfway between joints, indicates instinctive thinking by an experienced designer at a very early stage in the project development.

Designers working on the development of ideas will not necessarily require images describing surface qualities in great detail. That will exist in their imaginations and they will 'see' colour and materials in their black-and-white drawings. As they evolve their drawings, they are inevitably considering the nature of the surfaces they propose, and areas – apparently 'blank' to anyone else – will trigger the appropriate association in their mind's eye. However, they need to be careful not to indulge their imagination to the extent of speculating about impossible materials and unobtainable colours.

Freehand drawings such as these need not be big, no more than A4 – or any other size with which the maker is comfortable. Size can be adjusted with a colour photocopier or a scanner, and it is always useful to see what a change of scale can do to a drawing. Reduction will often lessen the impact of a weak area, while an increase in size can reveal enjoyable graphic incidents that are by-products of the media used. Textures and tones may be adjusted during reproduction.

FIRST

Below left and right
This model, made at 1:100
scale, with card less than a
millimetre thick, demonstrates
that a very small model can
effectively communicate crucial
three-dimensional information.
The vertical plane represents
the height of the existing space,
the new volumes are minimally
represented, but their interaction
is clear and the stair on the left is
convincingly described by a few
treads and its central structural
support.

Design models

When complex three-dimensional 'gestures' are proposed – for example, the addition of mezzanine levels and changes in ceiling heights – it is often productive to make a simple, very quick model. This can be rapidly assembled from plastic model-making sheet, cardboard, or even thick paper if the scale is small enough to eliminate large unsupported areas. Like sketches on paper, these models need not be well crafted, although, just as with the drawn sketch, frequent use will refine the technique and the quickly made model will take on a credibility that lends authority to the ideas it encapsulates. A convincing model, like a well-made sketch, will also foster the confidence of a designer in other aspects of the project.

Such exploratory models should be made as quickly as possible and the maker should be relaxed enough to pull them apart to incorporate the next stage of the design development. Elements can be held together with adhesive tape – or even pins.

Such models are 'works in progress' and their welfare is secondary to concerns for the outcome of the project. They can, like sketches, be used in early discussions with a client. The scruffiest examples can be made to look presentable when finger marks on grubby white card are spray-painted over.

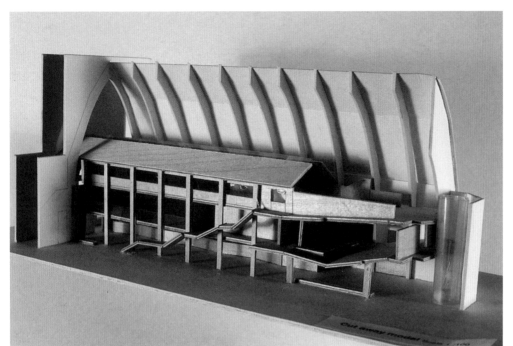

Left
Models can incorporate significant information about new and existing elements at early, exploratory design stages without needing to be finessed.

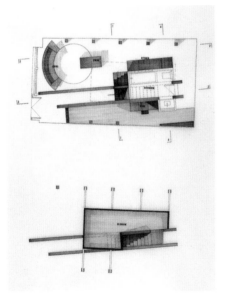

Above and above right
This model (above right), made from grey card with some added photocopied texture to represent significant changes of material, clarifies the plans (above). It also provides information about detail which can be ambiguous in two-dimensional drawings, like the slope of the top of walls around the stair and the expression of the stair profile on the other side of its supporting wall.

Right
Begun as a tool in the design process, this model has been upgraded for presentation purposes. It has been sprayed white to eliminate blemishes and additional detail has been added, such as the reception desk on the lower left and the stairs just appearing between the paired walls on the right. This all serves to make the comparative abstraction of the walls more understandable.

Detailed thinking

As a project progresses, a designer inevitably becomes increasingly concerned with detail.

Being precise

Every designer must learn to recognize the moment at which the means of investigating and progressing ideas must become more disciplined. It is often difficult to make the shift from the excitement of the first, comparatively unstructured, outpouring of ideas, when things move with an exhilarating momentum, regularly hinting at exciting possibilities, to the more considered scaled drawings which offer fewer options and more practical problems to deal with. Such reconsideration will inevitably happen at a slower pace because it requires objectivity, and changes are likely to impact on every other decision made up to that point. Usually such problems, however great their potential effect on the overall concept, will be small-scaled, a matter of reconciling a misalignment or an inadequate dimension, but their solution will take a disproportionate length of time and without their satisfactory solution the project will not achieve the honed perfection any decent designer should aspire to. Often, solutions necessitate changes in materials and methods of construction with a knock-on effect that takes time to assimilate into the whole, and generally the work necessary to create and refine any project will fill more than the time nominally available. The identification of a solution and examination of its impact on the rest of the project will require a heavy workload of precise and detailed drawing.

The most cherished drawings may well be the earliest. They will have the purest expression of the purest idea and may, superficially, appear to be the most creative. However, it is in the later, more considered, detailed drawings that the crucial creative work is done. Such drawings may appear dry, but they contain more hard information about the real nature of the project for those who know how to read them and it is often in consideration of detail that designers are forced into unfamiliar territory where habitual solutions must be abandoned and something new is added to their repertoire.

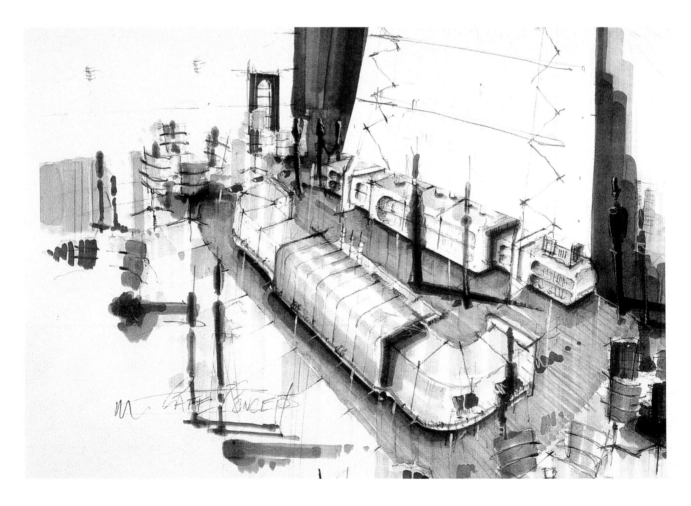

Above

Leather-covered furniture for a reception area was comparatively easy to draw both in plan and elevation. The technically constructed lines were then loosely over-drawn in pencil. The dense semi-matt black of the leather-and-chrome structure was rendered with oil pastels, and overshooting of edges integrated the image into the paper and created a contrasting background for the metal structure.

Opposite

Lines made with a thin black felt-tip pen and thicker coloured felt-tips on tracing paper express materials and surface qualities. The linear application of the coloured pens suggests floorboards and the hang of curtains. The grey tinting, particularly on the bar front and top suggests reflections on hard, shiny surfaces. The delineation of the bar is just enough to indicate how it operates, and the drawing is convincing because a sound practical knowledge underpins it. Critical decisions are, necessarily, taking shape in the designer's imagination.

Right

This sketch set out to consider light fittings for a café and, while considering the context for these, the designer began to speculate about crockery and cutlery. This particular speculation had a tangible outcome, but it is as likely that such peripheral drawing will have no useful result. However, whether productive or not, such thinking leads to an increasing sense of the totality of the interior.

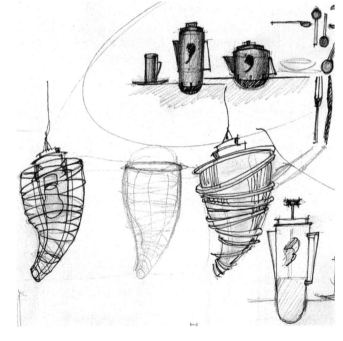

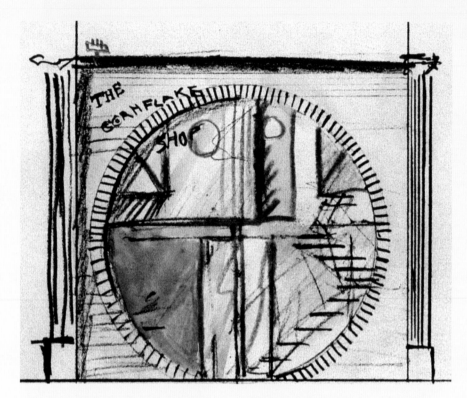

Left

An overlay, made on a technically drawn original, speculates about the position of the entrance door and brick patterning around the window.

This trio of drawings, made with pencil and coloured felt-tip pens on A4 sheets of tracing paper, chart the three-dimensional evolution of a complex interior. The drawings illustrated are the final overlays of sequences in which the designer was attempting to understand how free-standing elements at an upper level would exist and be accessed within the shell of the existing building.

The obvious speed with which the drawings were made, in an attempt to keep pace with, record and give shape to the thoughts that raced through the designer's imagination, is a convincing demonstration of how thinking and drawing are symbiotic, the one feeding and driving the other as early ideas merge with apparent spontaneity. There is enough evidence in these images to suggest that the designer draws with skill and authority but that, at this stage of the project, quality of drawing was secondary to generating and examining ideas.

The first drawing is primarily concerned with the street frontage, examining how the rectangular door might sit within the circle of the two-storey window and how the brick detailing might respond to the circle. The perfection of the circle makes it obvious that the basic form was made by overlaying a technically constructed original. There is some thought about how the interior elements would also relate to the circular window and colour is used to express their independence.

The rough outline of two walls of the existing building defines the interior space. The two light sources – the circular window and the triangular roof light at the rear – are indicated in recognition that they can together provide significant quantities of natural light which will, in turn, be dramatized by reflection and shadows as it interacts with the angular and rounded forms of the raised 'cabins'. The walkway that connects the 'cabins' is hinted at, and the possibility of a distinctive stair structure begins to emerge.

The geometry of the stair landing is the crucial element of the final drawing, after its essential form emerged in earlier, overlaid, versions. The remainder of the stair is represented skilfully but perfunctorily, a recognition that it can now only be resolved when drawn precisely to scale. The 'cabins' are drawn even more quickly but there is a suggestion that the designer is also beginning to think about details of doors, windows and finishes, all of which can also only be resolved in more carefully constructed drawings.

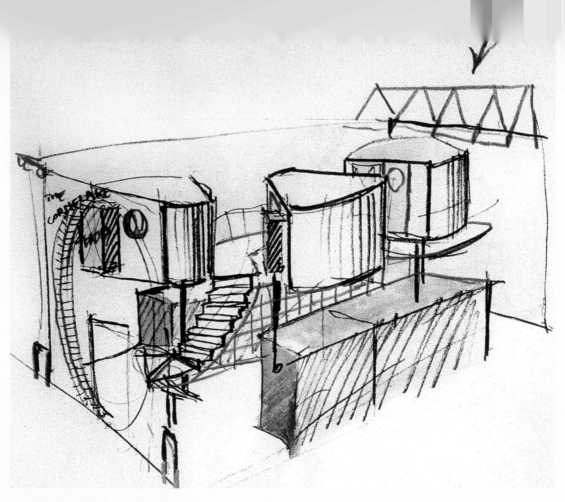

Above

An exploration of how the raised elements sit with the rectangle of the existing building shell.

Left

A much more detailed perception of the geometry of the stair establishes that the step incorporated into the landing provides a crucial definition of how the stair flights mirror each other and can sit comfortably within the corner of the existing shell.

While it is perhaps inevitable that most early drawings, which try to define the direction of a project, are speculative sketches, it is important that all drawings attempt to deal with the reality of the existing building; that they confront the difficulties it presents. Such drawings – plans, elevations and sections – should be to scale.

Below

One of a series of overlays, made with pencil on tracing paper. The significant elements in the existing structure, particularly the columns projecting from the side walls, are indicated so that decisions about the location of new elements are made in response to them. Floor pattern identifies the mezzanine area, but while the whole is drawn comprehensively there is little attempt to make it comprehensible for anyone other than the designer. Notes are scribbled and meant to serve as aides-mémoires rather than sources of information. The drawing is not refined and might be enough to serve for preliminary discussions but is more likely to end up in the wastebasket.

Right

This drawing – pencil and pastels on tracing paper – describes clearly the materials that will be used to make this façade (panels of timber strips and glass) and hints at the methods by which they may be assembled (nails and bolts). It suggests obvious questions about structural stability and the mechanics of the door, and in so doing points to the next step in the development of the project

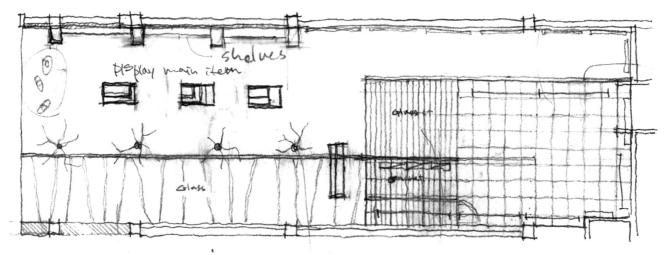

Drawing for the team

When designers sketch it is usually a private function in which they give some shape to their first thoughts, but the freehand sketch is also an efficient way of communicating with other members of the design team: colleagues and consultants.

Such drawings tend to be slightly more formal than a sketch that is made for personal consumption, because the designer's instinct will be to resolve ideas a little more before they are offered for discussion. They will be more intricate because they have to make their points clearly, and they will lack much of the exuberance of the spontaneous sketch because they must be as unambiguous as possible.

It makes sense to observe drawing conventions when making even the roughest sketches, otherwise they are open to misinterpretation by those familiar with normal practice. Plans are deemed to be drawn at 1.2 metres (4 feet) above floor level and those elements that stretch above this height, such as walls, are usually shown as solid blocks of tone, and those below in outline only. Elements above head height are shown with a dotted and dashed line.

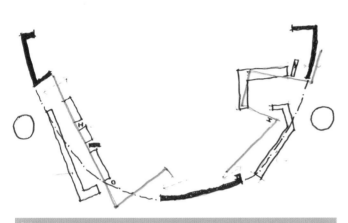

01
The plan is diagrammatic, traced over an existing plan. Elements are coded for clarity: unbroken black for the curved wall that rises from the floor and a dashed-and-dotted line for the sections above head height.

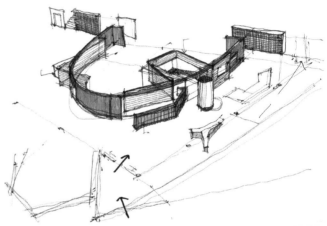

02
The three-dimensional view begins to clarify how the curved and angled walls interact in the vertical plane.

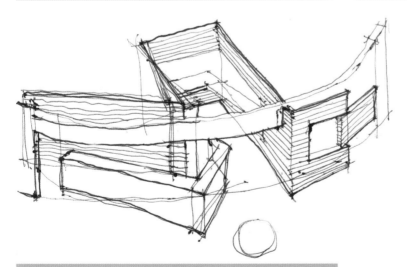

03
The third sketch looks in more detail at how the shop relates to the curved wall and the counter it shares with the box office. The shift in viewpoint offers a more expansive view of the inside of the shop.

Below and opposite

These drawings, good enough for first presentations to clients, retain some of the 'character' of the handmade image. The essential preliminary delineation by computer, including the scanning and pasting of advertising images, allowed a number of designers to add to the basic drawing without their individual freehand style becoming discordant. The larger figures were traced from photographs to ensure convincing body language.

The computer translates precise two-dimensional information in plan and section into three-dimensional images more accurately and significantly faster than can be done by hand. The initial image it produces will be exact, but is also very likely to be bland. The further refinement of that image by the addition of colour, materials and light using the computer will take time – particularly at an early stage in a project when definitive decisions that would justify fine-tuning have not yet been made. The 'base' drawings, created on computer, provide members of a team with an accurate perspective template, over which they may draw as individuals or as a team. Precision of line is maintained by the use of ruler, circle templates and 'French curves'.

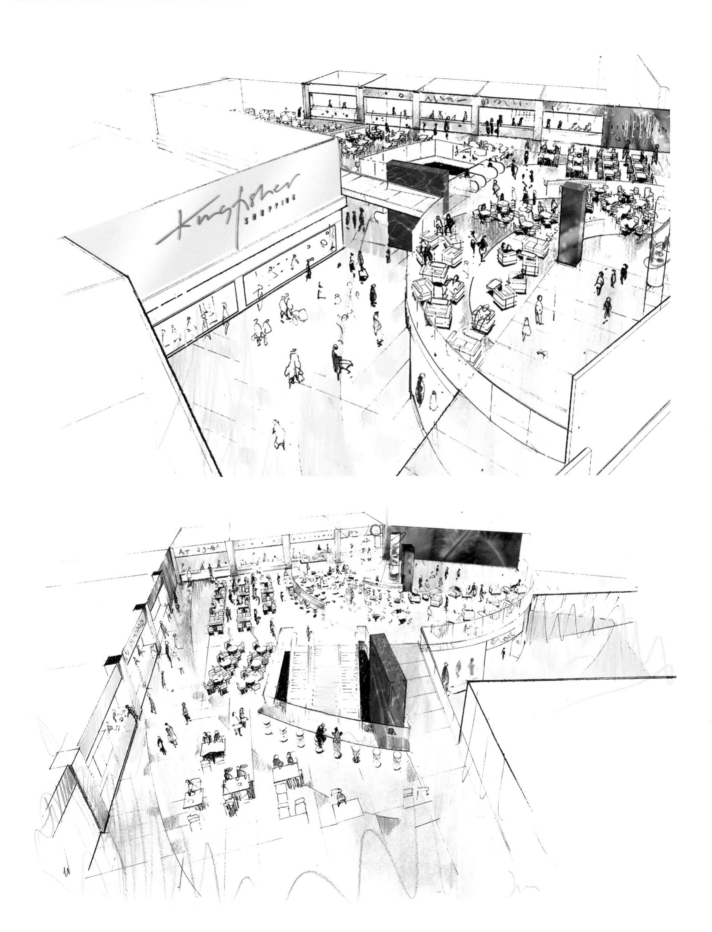

Below
'Freehand' sketch made on a
computer – giving a uniformity
of line not found in handmade
drawings.

Below right
In this speculation about an
enclosed volume within a stairwell,
the immediate context – that of
stair below, bridge and glazed wall
– are all delineated and rendered
by computer in convincing
perspective. The retention of
'hidden lines' ensures some of the
ambiguities of a handmade sketch,
but the image may be rotated and
scrutinized on-screen.

'Sketching' by computer

There is an assumption that sketching is only done by hand, and that it remains the quintessence of 'artistic' creativity. Such a perception confuses technique with quality, and ignores the fact that drawings made on computer can have the values – and even the ambiguities – of a handmade sketch. It is possible to make 'freehand' drawings with a computer using a digital pen, a mouse or a finger on a laptop keypad.

The computer, like any other drawing medium, determines both the way the hand moves across the drawing surface and the quality of the line made. While the experience of making the drawing is comparatively close to that of using a conventional pen or pencil, there is a fluidity of line that is the product of a digital stylus not being directly in contact with the 'paper'. There is also a uniformity of line quality which it is almost impossible – and probably not desirable – to achieve in a handmade drawing.

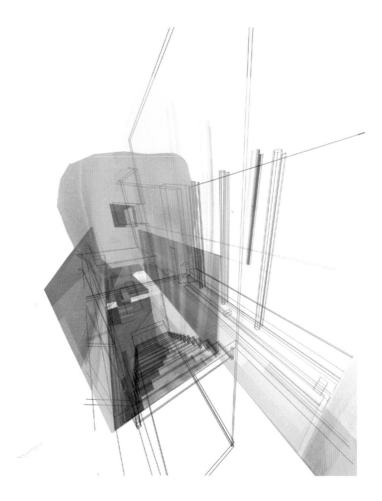

Right and below
The computer can create straight
lines and credible curves in two
and three dimensions, using
standard software 'tools'.

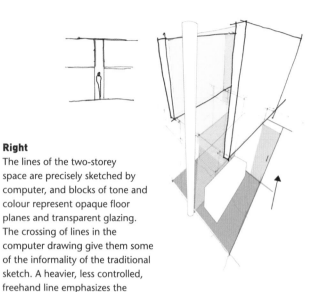

Right
The lines of the two-storey space are precisely sketched by computer, and blocks of tone and colour represent opaque floor planes and transparent glazing. The crossing of lines in the computer drawing give them some of the informality of the traditional sketch. A heavier, less controlled, freehand line emphasizes the contrast between rough walls and pristine glass.

Composites

Handmade and computer-generated images can coexist very successfully if each plays to their strengths. The skilled hand will give a relaxed and simple line, focusing of necessity on representing essentials; unless the computer is allowed to exploit its full potential for the complex representation of three-dimensional form, materiality and lighting, its output is likely to appear bland in comparison. The strengths of the two instruments may, however, be combined at all stages of the design process.

TIP COMPOSITES

A complex three-dimensional structure is convincingly represented by computer. The secondary content, the hanging garments that give it identity and explain its function, are suggested more tentatively with a skilful hand-drawn line that does not interfere with the powerful expression of the primary form.

Above
In the computer, it is simple to add colour, graded to suggest light, to a hand-drawn sketch.

Above left
Conversely, this computer-generated view is drawn over by hand in order to enrich the line quality of a minimal drawing – but then the blocks of colour, which add solidity, are added in the computer.

Right

The computer sets up the complex three-dimensional elements, but lines are drawn over for variety and colours are added by hand. Figures are introduced in order to explain how they interact with the red structures.

Below

It was important in this project to reinforce the perception of height within an atrium. The computer's capacity to create perfect perspective achieves this persuasively. Again, over-drawing and the addition of people take the image beyond the basic computer printout.

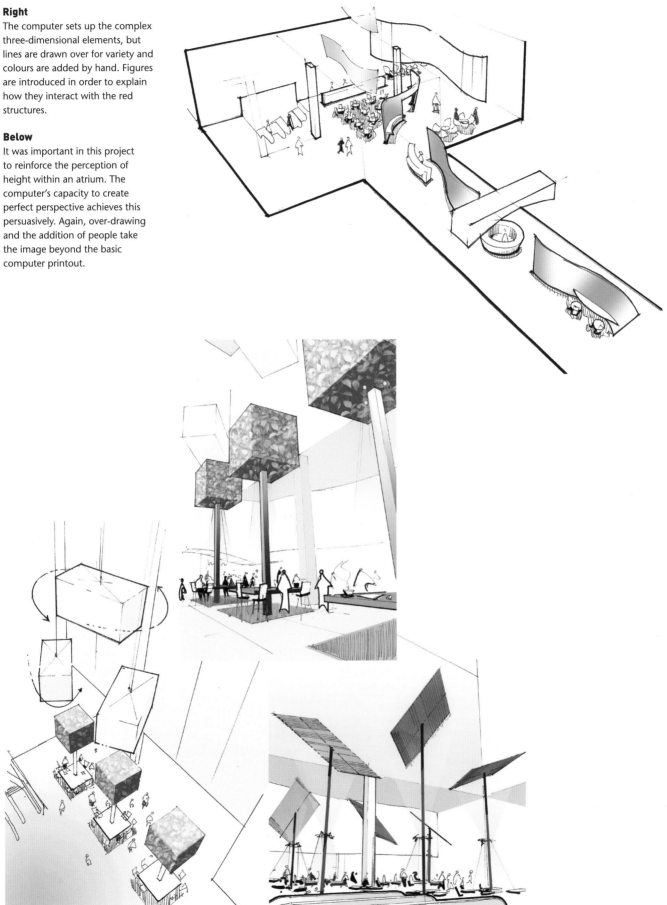

Developing ideas by computer

It is still generally conceded that at the earliest stages of the design process one will make quick freehand sketches, and for some designers – particularly those educated to use traditional techniques – this is, and will remain, true. However, for those who have used computers from the beginning of their training, and as an integral part of their practice and daily lives, it has become as easy to 'doodle' and 'sketch' on screen as on a drawing board. It remains a matter of personal preference, but there are, again, significant advantages to working digitally.

Once basic information has been fed into the computer, it becomes simple to generate outputs quickly and convincingly in two and three dimensions. The accuracy and clarity of the finished image ensure that, in contrast to freehand sketches, there is much less room for misinterpretation during discussion.

While a complex form may be drawn by hand, it is difficult – and frequently impossible – to translate such an image into the objective information needed for construction, but given the right software it is possible. For instance, linked CAD (computer-aided design) and CAM (computer-aided manufacture) equipment can convert ideas generated in two dimensions into the information necessary for manufacture. The inhibiting factor then becomes one of cost, rather than the difficulty of translating the abstract into the tangible.

01
An early elevation establishes the idea of of a ribbon stretching over a floor and up a wall.

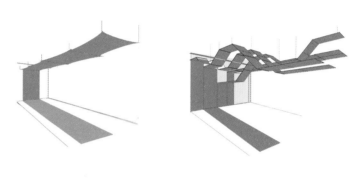

02
The idea is developed in three dimensions.

03
Walls, furniture and figures are added to establish context and decribe how the area might work.

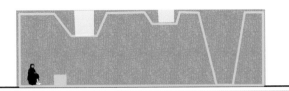

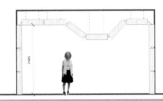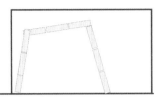

01
The section/elevation provides basic information, from which all subsequent drawings are generated. The figure identifies scale throughout the sequence.

02
The basic form remains consistent, but variations can be assessed quickly and objectively.

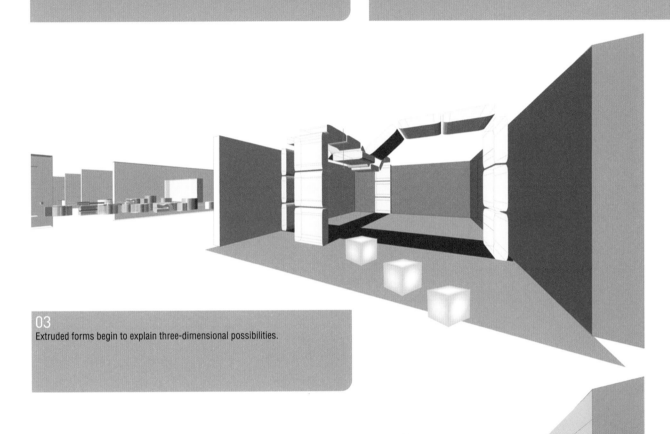

03
Extruded forms begin to explain three-dimensional possibilities.

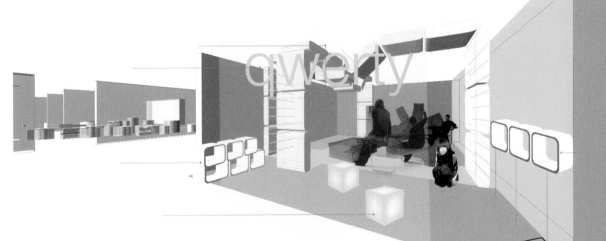

04
The computer also facilitates online access to material on manufacturers' websites, which may be downloaded to become an integrated component in the design process. Colours, to match paint or material samples, furniture and figures may be scanned and pasted into the image.

Olga Valentinova Reid has developed a way of generating images that present her with random options for consideration. While the images appear random, they are, she says, outcomes of the computer's 'logic' and therefore all have relevance, albeit tangentially, because they evolve from project data which has already been fed into the computer. If they do not provide 'answers', they certainly suggest possibilities – and do so in a visual language appropriate to the project.

The drawings shown below are a small fraction of those generated and the potential number is infinite. Valentinova Reid 'creates' the images by spontaneous selection of software functions, which progressively transform the starting point into something quite radically different and offer fresh perceptions that divert the imagination when it has become locked into unproductive linear paths. She acknowledges that the production of these variations can become self-indulgently prolific, but suggests that 'messy thinking is creative thinking' and that it is in the flurry of unanticipated variations on her theme that her imagination may find a stimulus.

Valentinova Reid points out that, if these two-dimensional forms are transported back to a three-dimensional drawing program, which is feasible with most softwares, then a designer has the opportunity to extrude shapes and begin to rationalize and translate the image into something that may be built. A designer's imagination will stubbornly try to translate the most arbitrary starting points into some kind of reality, speculating about appropriate materials and methods of construction.

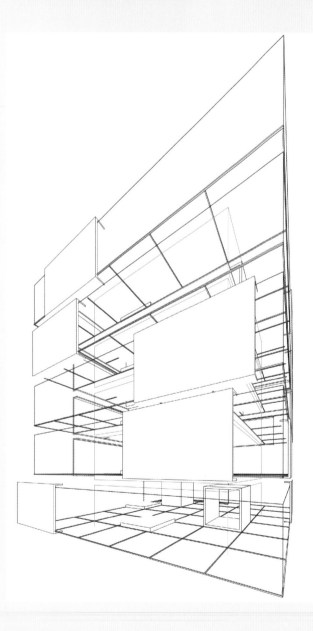
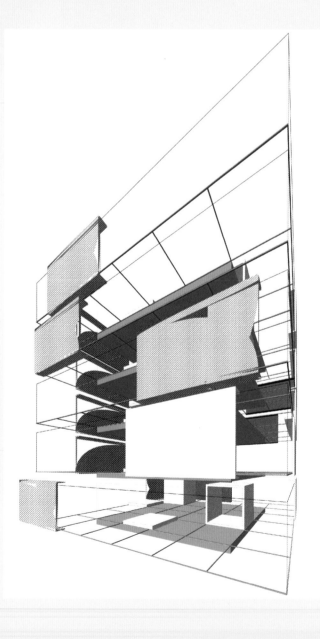

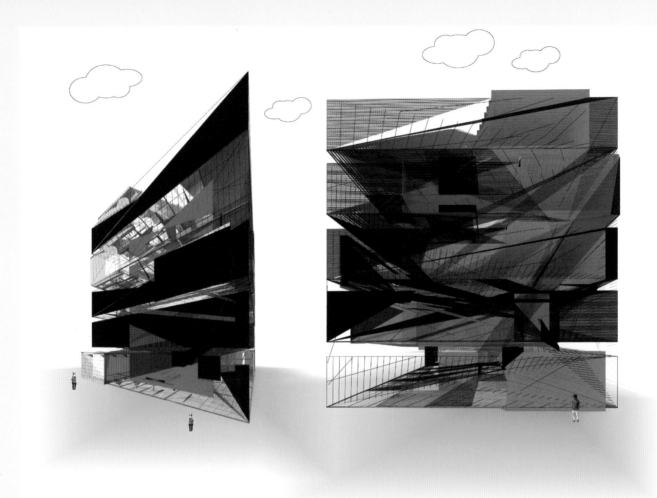

Opposite left

The image on the far left shows a variation on a section in which the computer has been 'prompted' to mutate the rational first visualizations of the project. It offers a glimpse of where the project might head, leaving the designer to consider its viability, speculating about appropriate materials and construction.

Opposite right

This more abstract image suggests, at one extreme, complex structures and, at the other, two- and perhaps three-dimensional patterns.

Above

The third and fourth images in this sequence show how the same technique can be used to develop colour options. Such shapes, generated during speculation about the nature of the project and critically assessed in that context, become the equivalent of traditional doodling – with the crucial difference that the doodling hand returns obsessively to reproducing the same familiar motifs, while these images, although they emerge organically from the project, are wholly unanticipated and continually offer new forms.

Chapter 3
Presentation

Presentation to clients and others

Presentation images and models are made to persuade the client, and sometimes others, of the desirability and credibility of a proposal. For most projects, the crucial approval is that of the client, who can make ideas that can otherwise only exist in a designer's imagination tangible. A good designer ought therefore to be able to find a way of meeting a client's needs and aspirations satisfactorily and satisfyingly, however antipathetic they may at first appear.

Approval is also often necessary from the statutory bodies responsible for giving formal, legal permission. If this is refused at the first attempt, there is little opportunity to appeal against verdicts or to make adjustments because the timescale for interior projects is usually short. Planners will be primarily interested in street frontages, but they will also want to know about changes to protected historical interiors.

A client will often rent premises, and the building's owners will want to approve proposed alterations. Owners of retail developments will have to fulfil conditions, with which all leaseholders must comply. These are seldom onerous, but they will be mandatory.

Presentation to a client, or any other interested parties, is not necessarily a one-off event. It is prudent to talk to all parties during the progression of the design process in order to ensure that protracted, unproductive work is avoided. Fine-tuning of a brief is frequently necessary. The nature of interior design, working within the restrictions of the shell of an existing building, means that, almost inevitably, the detail of an initial brief will have to be reconsidered in response to emerging realities. Clients who accept significant financial risks deserve to be consulted at all stages and, as proposals are scrutinized, other possibilities will suggest themselves and changes

of direction must be discussed and agreed. It therefore makes sense to set up a series of preliminary presentations in order to consider and agree on work in progress.

Presentations should take into account the knowledge, preconceptions and prejudices of those for whom they are intended. Some will be impressed by the 'artistic' quality of drawings, while others will be reassured by evidence of technological expertise. They all ought to be able to understand everything to which they are being asked to agree. Shortcomings may be glossed over temporarily, but they will become blatantly apparent when the work is complete and making them right will be expensive and embarrassing. The extent of a client's ability to understand the various types of drawings that can make up a presentation will become obvious in early conversations.

When a client is familiar with a designer's work – or when the two have collaborated before – it may be appropriate to produce fewer, and perhaps less-polished, drawings, but it must not appear that the client is being taken for granted and receiving less for their fee. Some clients enjoy the sense of collaboration in the development of ideas and will tend to prefer the less-polished drawings that suggest work in progress. With new clients it is obviously important to make an impression – perhaps even to offer a little more than is strictly necessary, and certainly no less. Evidence of enthusiasm and ability will overcome most reservations.

Successful presentation material

Designers tend to be fascinated by clients' response to presentations, particularly to individual drawings within the whole, and are always keen to identify the one illustration that swung the argument – often reminiscing later about how a single, seductive image persuaded a client to find extra money.

The tone of any presentation, particularly during the face-to-face encounter with the client, depends very much on the personality of the designer. Some have natural gravitas and can easily convince clients of their serious intent and reliability, while others are instinctively inclined to humour and to finding a more personal level of communication. Whatever the inclination, it will be manifested in both visual and verbal presentations. Both positions, and any in between, will be drastically undermined by a blatant error in any drawing.

Opposite
Two drawings from a set of 14, both showing different areas within a shopping development, focus client attention on the distinctive elements of each and provide comprehensive material for detailed discussion.

Above right
The plan on the right is supported by a collage of snapshots to illustrate the existing office space's practical shortcomings.

Right
The initial drawing is a plan of the existing office, but the text – instead of identifying areas which are already well known to the clients – describes the space's practical shortcomings.

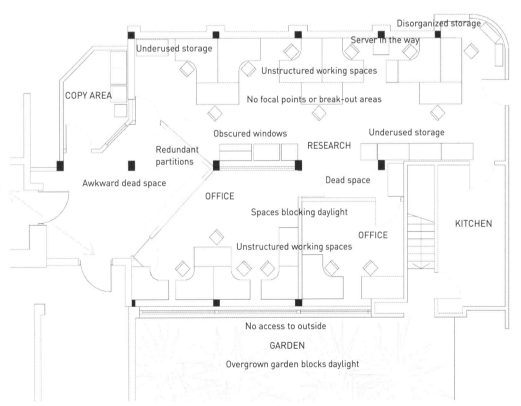

Disorganized storage
Underused storage
Server in the way
Unstructured working spaces
COPY AREA
No focal points or break-out areas
Obscured windows
RESEARCH
Underused storage
Redundant partitions
Dead space
Awkward dead space
OFFICE
Spaces blocking daylight
KITCHEN
OFFICE
Unstructured working spaces
No access to outside
GARDEN
Overgrown garden blocks daylight

The following example of presentation material resulted in the clients' agreement and commitment to the project. The first examples (this page) were presented at an early client meeting.

The next two pairings (opposite) offer alternatives to the clients. Frequently, although not in this case, the client will suggest a solution incorporating elements of some or all of the options offered. This may be irritating to designers, but it helps identify priorities.

The computer provides credible perspective, but hand-drawn details are necessarily simplified and require extra definition. The collage comprising scanned photographs of elements from other, completed, interiors suggests some of the anticipated qualities of the project. The individual illustrations, particularly of the chairs, provide evidence of the high standard of drawing in the sketches and suggest that the designer is in control of all aspects of the creative process. There is always a danger that over-indulgent use of found images will distort clients' expectations, and it is sensible to use illustrations from one's own completed projects where possible.

Top and above
Option 1, described as the 'low-impact concept', demonstrates how a minimal tidying of the plan and the introduction of new furniture would improve the workspace. The perspective, set up on computer, is over-drawn by hand, and colours and tones are then added on computer.

Right and below

Option 2, or the 'full concept', uses the same techniques and the plans are similar. However, the perspective view now illustrates the whole of the office because the entire area is reconfigured, giving the outdoor area prominence. The plan demonstrates a much more rational and efficient solution, identifying and exploiting the neglected potential of the existing space. The designer's own preference for this version is perhaps indicated by the more extensive pencil work embellishing the raw computer lines. The clients also decided to go for this option.

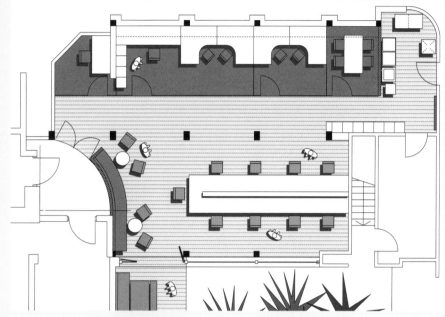

Some projects are won in competition. In these cases, the strategy must be slightly different because the designers may not have an opportunity to talk to the judges.

Sometimes a commissioning client may not be a user of the space. Often, particularly with work for public bodies, the client will be a committee – not usually an easy body with which to negotiate. There is no single individual to respond to, and there may be tensions within the group which make differences of opinion – even differences unrelated to the proposal – inevitable. In such circumstances, things must be kept clear and simple. Often laypersons are concerned that they will be unable to understand specialist drawings and are anxious about looking foolish. Such anxieties can make them reluctant to engage with the material presented and hesitant about expressing opinions and approval. Accessible drawings supported by a relaxed, preferably good-humoured, verbal presentation can begin to overcome this.

The competition entry shown on these pages, for an exhibition structure, was presented on A3 sheets, which committed the judging panel to concentrating on one idea at a time. The drawings were straightforward in order to complement the theme of recycling simple, basic units.

Left
A sequence of drawings illustrating some of the options offered by the basic components of an exhibition system.

TIP DRAWINGS FOR INTERIM PRESENTATIONS

Drawings should be:
- Simple and informal
- Comprehensible without appearing definitive
- Realistic – don't hint at something that can't be delivered
- Quick – elaborate presentations consume time and therefore cost money

Right
This image illustrates the strategy for delivering light and power to a typical configuration of basic components.

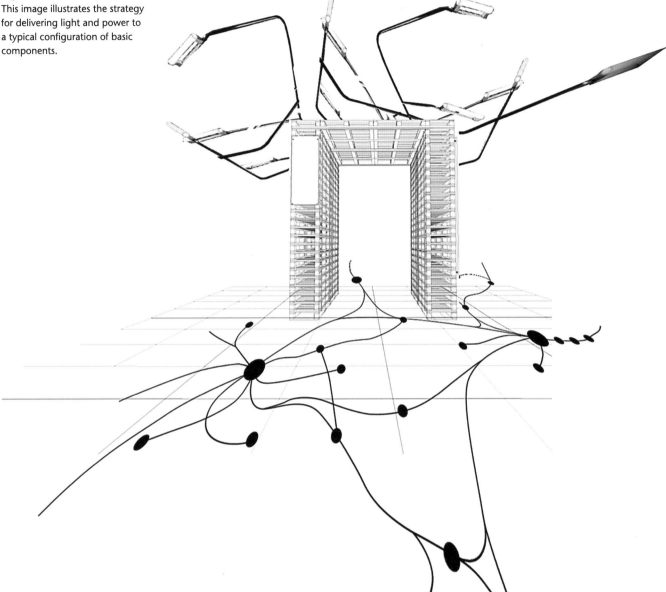

The components of a presentation

Whether for preliminary or final presentations, there are a number of standard types of drawings – each with its own defining conventions – that will necessarily be produced for most projects.

The character of drawings, whether technical or not, is always determined by the medium with which they are made. Drawings for interior design need to be precise.

When drawing by hand, different weights of line, in the case of pencil, and thicknesses, in the case of pen, help legibility. The use of colour was generally restricted to one-off drawings until the advent of effective colour photocopying. Definition of elements within the drawing required laborious hatching and toning before the advent of computer-aided design. Computer drawing and printing now makes it easy to use colour and infinite shades of grey. The computer's richer palette offers a battery of options for the creation of more accessible drawings. However, it is important not to obscure crucial facts with an overload of colour and texture.

While the perspective view may be perceived as the quintessential presentation tool, other, less spectacular, two-dimensional drawings convey crucial information more clearly.

The plan

A plan is usually essential. It defines how the required accommodation is deployed and confirms that it fits into the existing space.

Plans may, of necessity, be visually complex. It is, therefore, often good practice to use a diagrammatic version of the plan, explaining how the essential elements are arranged, as an introduction to a more complex version that incorporates more comprehensive and detailed information.

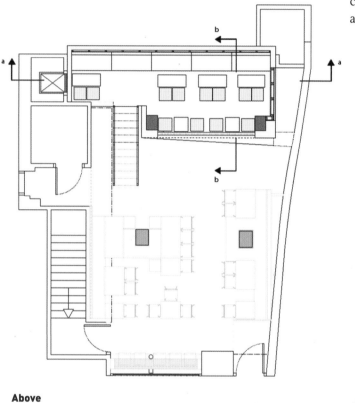

Above

A simple plan of a mezzanine level, in which the computer's capacity to add tone and colour is exploited in order to clarify information. The grey-toned areas represent the walls enclosing the mezzanine and, in the lower half of the drawing, the two columns which rise through the double-height space. A new wall is tinted orange, and upholstered seating pink.

Right

Detailed delineation is enriched by the computer's capacity to deal immaculately with tones, colours and text. Tone in the smaller plan explains the zoning of activities. The addition of furniture and equipment in the larger version confirms that the uncompromising planning delivers efficient spaces.

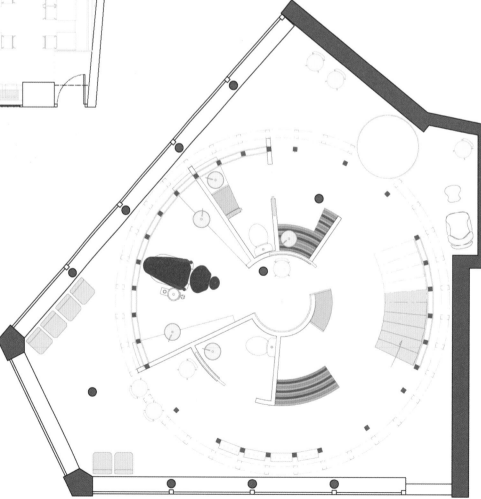

TIP SCALES

There are standard scales for drawings, recognized throughout the building industry. Generally, 1:50 is most useful for presentation plans: it is big enough to show a comprehensive amount of detail and to allow most projects to be contained on a single page. A scale of 1:100 is also capable of providing significant information, particularly with the precision and quality of line possible on a computer, but a 1:200-scale plan begins to lose important detail. If a comprehensive plan of a large project is necessary and may only be achieved at 1:200, then areas that are densely organized, or of particular interest, may be dealt with at a larger scale, say 1:50 or 1:20. The capacity of the computer to alternate easily between scales makes this conversion simple.

The scale of a plan should be declared on the drawing, but when a scale is used for which there is no 'ruler' – and therefore no way of measuring the paper copy – it should be declared to be 'not to scale' in a prominent position somewhere on the sheet.

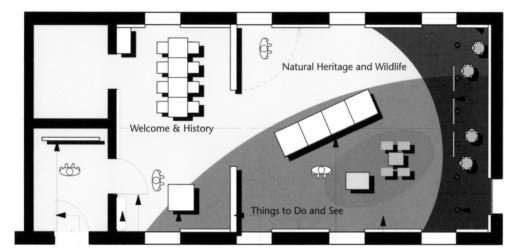

Natural Heritage and Wildlife

Welcome & History

Things to Do and See

Left
This plan for an exhibition also works as a diagram, because the space is simple and contains few elements or items of equipment. The floor pattern dominates, as it would in the finished interior, and identifies the different areas. The detailed specification notes relate easily to their subjects without confusing the plan, and the furniture layout confirms that the spaces work.

Right
Solid black represents existing structure, and white indicates the new walls. Other colours refer to floor finishes. Tonal variations suggest the impact of artificial lighting. 'Shadows', cast by the round tables, and the graded colour on the green ramp add a degree of three-dimensionality.

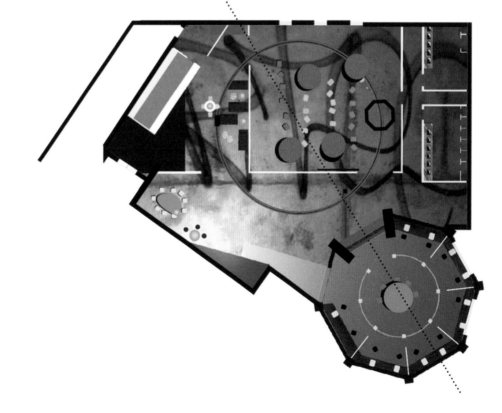

Below

Tracing over a measured survey
ensures that dimensions are
accurate to an acceptable degree.
Fast freehand drawing makes
shading and indications of
furniture layout easy.

Below right

This project involves more
detailed work, and consequently
the drawings are more accurate.
A drawing pen was used in
preference to a pencil, because it
ensured precision and permanence
of line. The black ink outline was
drawn on tracing paper, which
was then tinted on the back with
coloured pencils. New walls and
columns were coloured orange
to clarify the modest extent of
construction work. Other lines and
colouring represented floor finishes
and furniture layouts. The plans
of the three floors were butted
together, and distinguished by
different densities of tone.

Handmade plans

Near perfection of line can be achieved by someone
constantly making technical drawings by hand, but the
hand can never match the extraordinary precision of the
computer, its consistency of line and its perfect corners.
It is therefore logical, when drawing by hand, to aim
for a more 'relaxed' outcome: to allow lines to cross, for
example, and to apply hatching and toning vigorously,
perhaps to suggest a certain creative exuberance.

For some simple projects drawing may be done
freehand, without the use of T-square or set square.
Corners, usually close to ninety degrees, may be judged
by eye, and practice will improve this skill. Significant
dimensions may be measured, even in a freehand drawing
and, if these are comparatively accurate, other elements
may be drawn credibly in relation to them.

For more complex plans, an alternative is to create
a quick, technically constructed draft of the crucial
elements and then to make a freehand overlay. It is not
advisable to trace the original too carefully, because
with most of the drawing being accurate the inevitable
minor discrepancies will appear clumsier in comparison.
It is generally better to trace quickly in order to sustain
spontaneity. Technically constructed and freehand lines
may usefully be employed in the same drawing – the first
can define the precision of new elements, and the second
the imprecision of existing features.

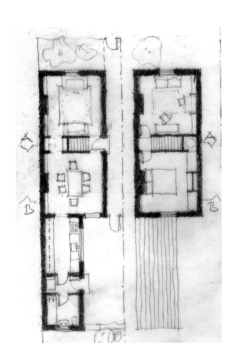

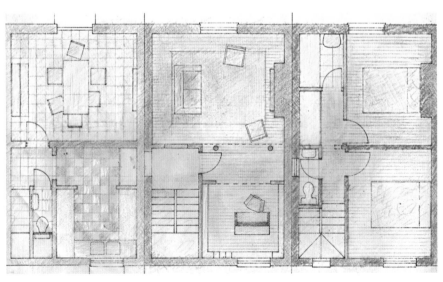

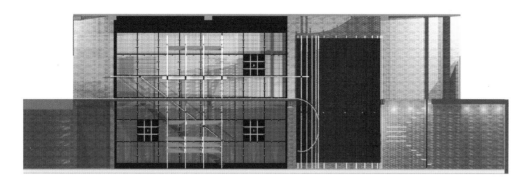

Left
Developed rendering of materials can give an impression of materiality, colours, texture and light.

Below left
It tends to be normal practice to people drawings with glamorous models, and such superhumans sit incongruously in most interiors. In this meticulously detailed image there is a much more eclectic and engaging collection of 'characters'.

The section

All the observations made about drawing plans apply equally to the section. The section is the essential way to accurately describe changes of level, whether at floor or ceiling levels, because the sense of depth and projection become ambiguous in perspective views.

It can be counterproductive to be overly conscientious when drawing sections. If too many lines are incorporated, in order to represent background detail, the whole becomes difficult to decipher. When planning the drawing, it is important to decide on priorities and to edit out insignificant information.

A section can offer a prosaic description of the physicality of a space or can evoke atmosphere with accurate descriptions of colour, materials, lighting effects and furniture.

If the plan allows a viewer to navigate and understand the topography of a space, the section describes its vertical planes and allows an understanding of their composition as the viewer 'moves' through the space. The computer's capacity for precise representation of finishes makes it the ideal tool for this job.

The crucial decision, which will determine whether a section is useful or not, is that about the location of its 'cut' through the building. This should ensure that the subsequent drawing includes the information most essential for describing the project. It is usually good practice to make a number of sections, each dealing with a significant condition, rather than to attempt the false economy of superimposing one on the other. Generally speaking, one section should cut through a stairwell in order to explain, practically and aesthetically, how floors connect. It is also imperative to cut through the edge of any mezzanine floor, to describe changes and visual links between levels.

There is also a choice to be made about the direction in which a section ought to 'look'. It should obviously be orientated to place elements in the most informative context or to incorporate information about an important background element.

Introducing people and props can give scale to a section and help explain how the interior will be used. Well-chosen figures can assist in making otherwise forbidding technical drawings appear more accessible.

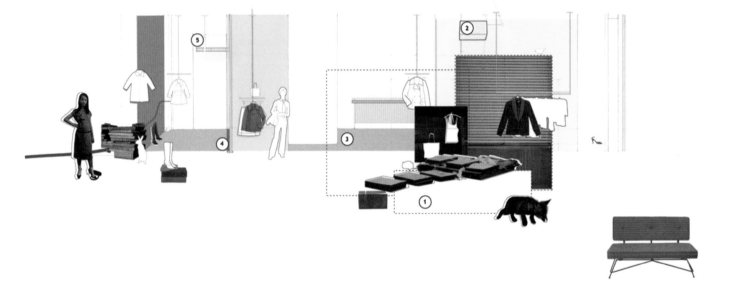

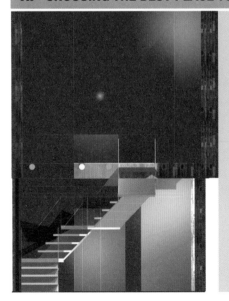

TIP CHOOSING THE BEST PLACE TO 'CUT' THE SECTION

It is always informative to draw a section through a stairwell because it shows the vertical interaction of levels. This example also deals with the impact of colour and light; the glass balustrades are outlined for clarity.

Above

While not a traditional section, the coloured elements describe the essential components of a minimalist clothes shop. The projection of these elements beyond the strict confines of the section plane introduces a sense of depth. The sparse precision of the whole is relieved by the, perhaps ironic, intrusion of wildlife.

The axonometric and the isometric

Plans and sections allow navigation of a space but in strictly two-dimensional terms, and the perspective presents a fixed viewpoint. Axonometric and isometric projections are essentially three-dimensional views of all areas within a building, with its roof and at least two walls removed. They provide a method of constructing images that exhibit the virtues of both two and three dimensions.

They are simple to construct, and explain the translation of plans and sections into three dimensions. They allow the viewer to imagine moving around the space, or sequence of spaces; to understand how one area flows into another; and how the aesthetics of one evolve into another. A viewpoint must be selected in order to ensure that the maximum information is offered, and it is often sensible to draw a project from more than one viewpoint – usually from diagonally opposite corners, to provide an even spread of information

Obviously, it is simple to generate a number of such images electronically once information about plan and section conditions have been fed into the computer. It is also comparatively easy to set them up by hand because lines run in parallel rather than in the constantly changing divergences of the perspective view. This uncomplicated formula makes it feasible to draw axonometrics and isometrics quickly and with a satisfactory degree of accuracy by hand, such that they can be an effective way of making three-dimensional sketches during the course of a meeting. (For the principles of setting them up, refer to the section on 'Axonometric and isometric projections' in Chapter 1, pages 42–43.)

Below left
In this computer-generated illustration three-dimensional organization is made clear, and meticulous rendering convincingly describes finishes.

Below
When made by hand, three-dimensionality is defined primarily by outline and, while every surface is rendered with pastels and coloured pencils, it is impossible to achieve the same accuracy in the depiction of materials.

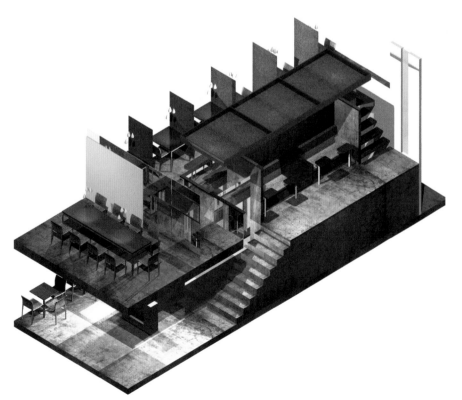

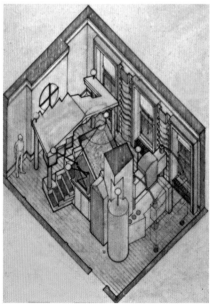

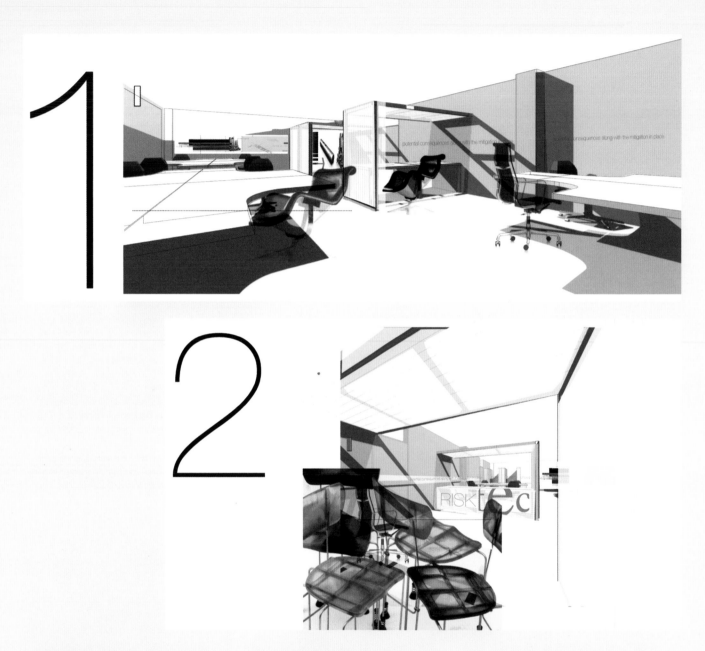

This presentation uses only computer-generated images and, because there are no changes to the existing office layout, offers only three-dimensional views. The clients were obviously familiar with the context, and ideas were discussed on site.

Furniture is downloaded from manufacturers' websites and, because of the accuracy that this process gives, supporting photographs of furniture are not required. The sequence of images explain how the areas work.

The overall images are, however, presented as work in progress: deliberately simple, suggesting possibilities, leaving room for discussion and, crucially for work on a comparatively modest budget, being quick to produce. The location of the identifying numbers works cleverly with the content of the images: '1' trims the side of the first, the horizontal bar of '2' lines through with the purple text, the shape of '3' is echoed in the chairs, '4' locks into the wall shown in elevation and '5' reflects the curved structure.

The designer's, and ultimately the client's, preference was for option 1. This is not unusual, because an experienced designer will have a sound instinct for the appropriate solution and their first idea is often the most appropriate. Nevertheless, other possibilities and variations on the first idea occur, and these have to be investigated. In this case the client was also excited by option 4, and the designer by 5. Discussion of alternatives gives both parties an appreciation of the other's position, and affords

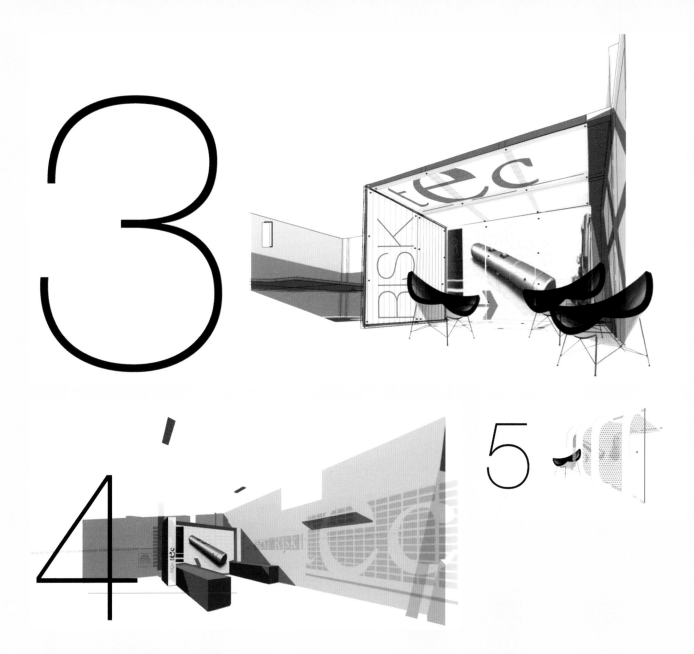

the client greater confidence about final decision-making. Any designer who has investigated a range of possibilities is also likely to be more confident that the final decision is the right one, and such confidence is important in the effective progression of the project. The effort to develop options is seldom wasted, because ideas that emerge in one project remain part of a designer's vocabulary and may be productively reworked in other contexts.

All images
Prominent identifying numbers act as a clever visual feature of this sequential client presentation.

Right

This sequence of three images documents a strategy for the construction of an enclosed office space, demonstrating that what is an apparently complex structure may be built using familiar materials and construction techniques.

Below

A description of a continuous element that runs the length of a long, narrow building, progressively changing its function but not its character. The drawing is simplified, but remains detailed enough to explain the essential idea. The omission of external walls and floor focuses attention on the new elements.

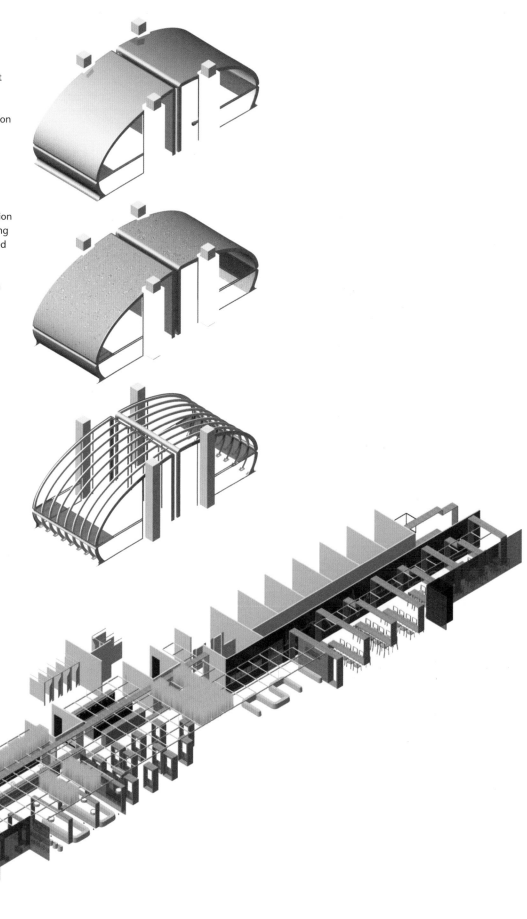

The difficulty with an image dealing with a number of levels often lies in the integration of the staircase, which exists on and between each level. The drawings shown on this page explain three-dimensional interaction within a multi-level space with a staircase. The solution the designer of this project has arrived at is to isolate the staircase from both floors (here, it is the dark red element). Remnants of the curved, sloping brown wall that contains the staircase appear on both levels and indicate how these elements lock together. The void left on the upper plan by the stairwell identifies its location. The image is further clarified when read in conjunction with the perspective view shown below. Individual drawings in a presentation are frequently interdependent, the particular focus of each contributing to an understanding of the whole.

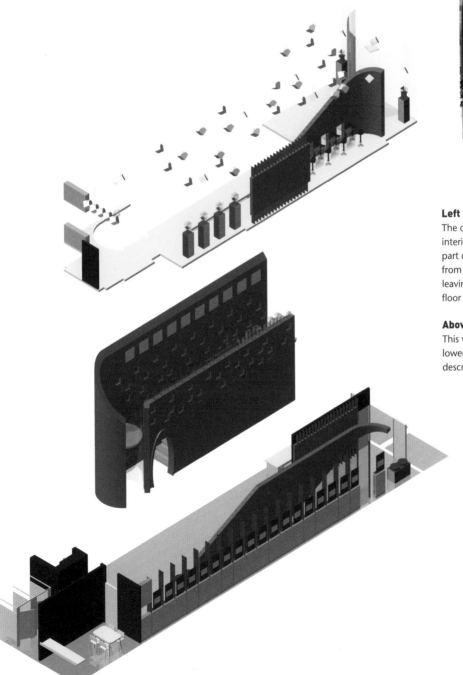

Left

The dark red wall occurs on both levels of the interior that contains the stair. In the central part of the diagram the stair volume is removed from each level and hovers between the two, leaving a void on the upper level and an empty floor on the lower level.

Above

This view of the entrance to the stair at the lower level confirms its location and further describes the spaces its presence creates.

For a computer, it is no more difficult to draw a curved line than a straight one – or a perspective than an axonometric. Using electronic means, it is therefore possible – when appropriate – to use the slightly more naturalistic overhead perspective view rather than an axonometric. For very complex spaces, however, the formal logic of the axonometric is likely to be more informative.

Above
This overhead view explains how elements sit within a double-height space. The image is necessarily complex, but clearly contrasts the fragility of the stair and connecting bridges with the enclosed workplaces.

Right
This overhead view veers away just enough from the true plan to indicate how colour and materials are used to express the interaction of the walls. The furniture indicates how areas will be used. Crucial elements of the exterior walls, such as windows and columns, are indicated on the edges.

The perspective

Elaborately detailed and polished perspective views are generally the key, most accessible images in any presentation, quickly conveying the essential elements of the project. One comprehensive perspective may express all that needs to be shown, but it is always worth considering a number of views, each concentrating attention on different important elements. Such shifts of attention are, after all, the normal response to a built interior, the eyes focusing consecutively on particular set pieces. It is also worth considering incorporating large-scale views of details, junctions of materials and pieces of built-in furniture. Such detail can create a sense of intimate involvement with the project. (For the principles of setting up perspective views, refer to the section on 'Making a simple freehand perspective' in Chapter 1, pages 38–40.)

The advantage of drawing by computer is that, once essential information has been fed into plans and elevations, it is comparatively simple to extrude as many complex perspective views as is necessary or desirable. A disadvantage, however, is that with too many such views the impact of the whole becomes diluted. It is better to identify those that are crucial, and invest effort in refining them.

Above
It makes sense to include a new street frontage as the first image in presentation material.
This may be viewed as an elevation, or . . .

Left
. . . as a perspective. The computer makes it easy to manipulate a new elevation to match the perspective of a, preferably digital, photograph of surrounding buildings. The latter may, in turn, be further manipulated within the computer to produce a more compatible alignment.

Right and below
The most complex proposals may
be easily and endlessly rotated in
the computer for critical appraisal
and presentation.

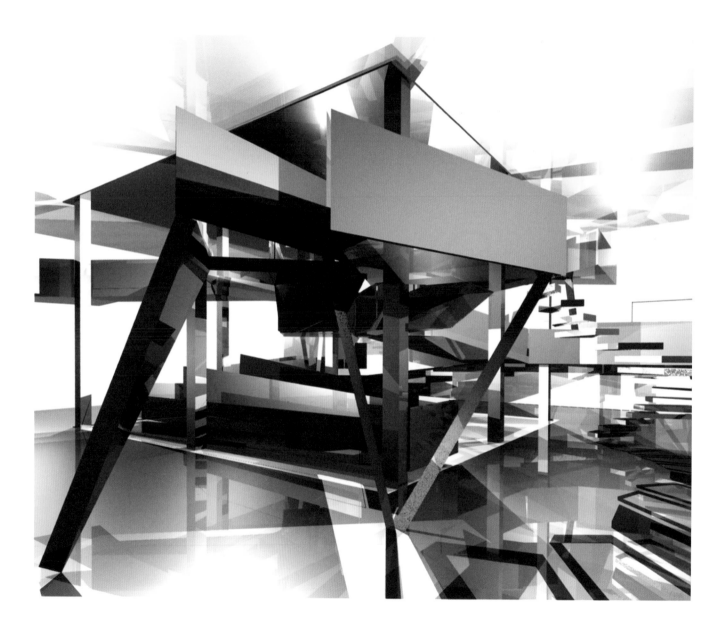

Right

At first sight, this image appears photographic: its concern is to convey a sense of machined perfection, so the surfaces are hyper-smooth and the whole is dramatically lit. Such distortion is legitimate in order to express the spirit of the project – as long as the manipulation is obvious.

Left

Artificial transparency indicates obvious stylization, and in this example also expresses the spirit of the project.

Building an interior is necessarily a more difficult undertaking than generating an idealized image of it. If a rendering appears perfect, then a client may be entitled to assume that the materials and colours shown are precisely those that will appear in the finished interior – and any variations may lead to complaints. It is therefore sometimes sensible to offer a more impressionistic image of the proposal.

These images explain how a palette of materials and colours runs consistently through a sequence of spaces. Created 'freehand' on computer, they describe finishes without the time-consuming precision necessary to plot three-dimensional detail. Important elements, like the clothes-hanging recesses and sculpted ceilings, are delineated carefully, but the obviously deliberate discrepancies of size in the figures, as well as their extreme postures and costumes, confirm that literal accuracy is not intended.

The conventional perspective view, neatly composed within a rectangle, tends, like a photograph, to give equal weight to all elements within it, whereas in a real interior one is more likely to focus on the visually significant. Similarly, in a drawing it is sensible to concentrate attention on the most significant elements, which can be lost if every surface is rendered with the same intensity. Content should be prioritized.

A strong argument can be made for computer-generated images that retain elements of the sketch. Sketches are always intriguing: they are not definitive, they leave room for the imagination to speculate – and they have spontaneity, energy and an intimacy that the perfection of the polished image has inevitably lost. They remain accessible.

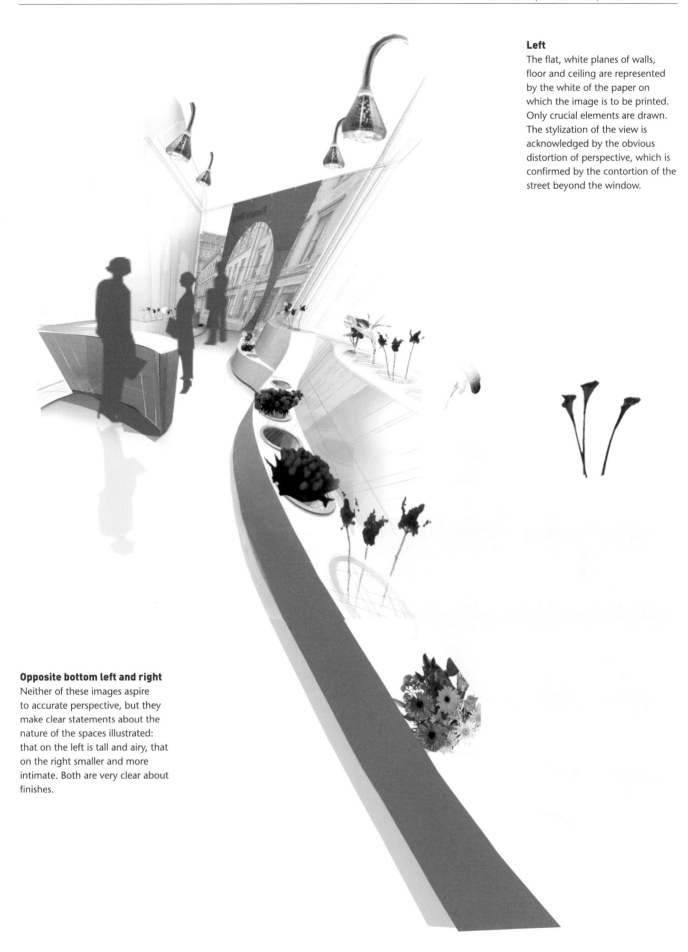

Left
The flat, white planes of walls, floor and ceiling are represented by the white of the paper on which the image is to be printed. Only crucial elements are drawn. The stylization of the view is acknowledged by the obvious distortion of perspective, which is confirmed by the contortion of the street beyond the window.

Opposite bottom left and right
Neither of these images aspire to accurate perspective, but they make clear statements about the nature of the spaces illustrated: that on the left is tall and airy, that on the right smaller and more intimate. Both are very clear about finishes.

Image edge

In built interiors, the eye focuses on the area directly in the line of sight and registers less precisely elements at the edge of the cone of vision. It will be drawn to, and linger on, the dominant elements, and while areas of peripheral vision contribute to the impression of the whole they will not be scrutinized with the same intensity.

An irregularly shaped image also breaks up the predictable grid that results when a number of rectangular images are collected on a presentation sheet.

Left

The partial retention of wire-frame lines allows the intensity of rendering to reduce from left to right. The drawing fades into the paper, and the lines help define individual elements.

Below

The white dotted lines, like the framing device in a camera viewfinder, define the area of interest and, along with the floating pink rectangle behind and the figures overstepping the edges of the images, enhance the sense of depth.

Right

The projection of the lines of the wire frame integrate the image into the page. However, the lines, while they obviously belong to the project, are not aligned precisely with the image and their disjunction suggests that it floats above the surface of the paper. The legs of the chair, also projecting beyond the strict confines of the image, increase the sense of depth.

Below right

The centre of this image is the most solidly rendered area, and tones fade as they 'rise' from it. It is an impossible view, but it deals with a tiny space and the main purpose of the drawing is to describe the finishes.

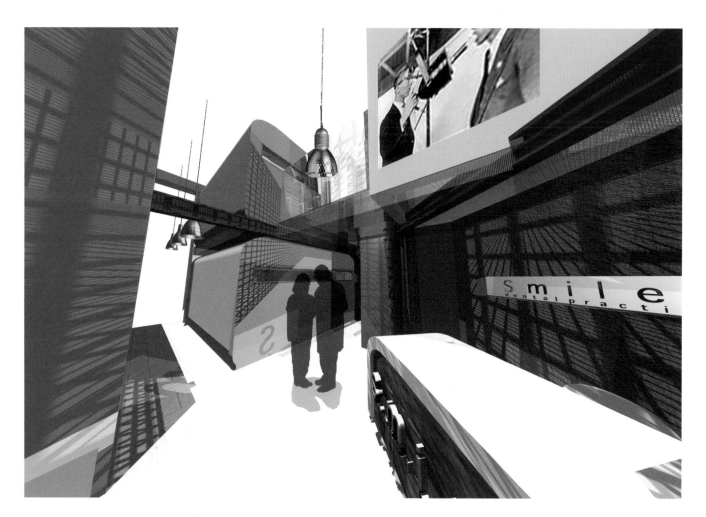

Opposite top and bottom

By omitting floors and ceilings, the white of the paper is allowed to cut through these images. As a result, while an edge is clearly implied the elements, particularly the green structure in the top image, have a strong sense of 'space' around them – something that tends to be lost when one rendered surface is set against another.

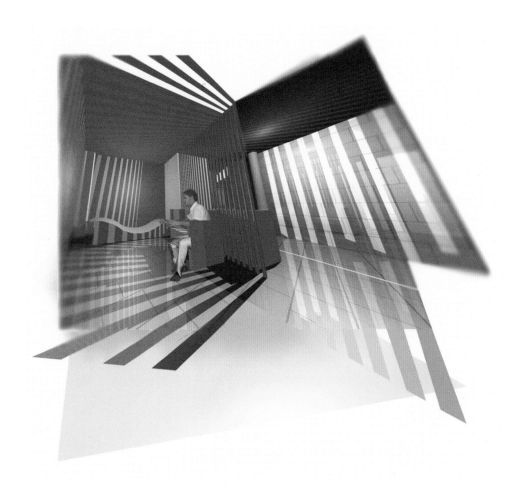

Above

The angled linearity of strips and shadows is centred around the core of the curved chaise longue, and held within a pale pink square that is just visible against the white of the paper.

Left

This image is stripped back to an expression of finishes and a suggestion of planes. Colours and pattern are complemented by the foreground figure. The line on the floor links the two principal areas. The heavier, right-hand, side is balanced by the floating triangular shape on the upper left.

Proposed finishes

It is common, and somewhat glib, to say that interior design is 'about space'. It is as much – and probably a great deal more – about surface, colours and textures. Since interior 'spaces' are usually rectangular and typically around 2.5 metres (8 feet) high, they depend for their success more on the creative handling of surface finishes than on dramatic sculptural gestures. Furthermore, no matter how well such 'sculpture' is handled, the way it is perceived will depend on the materials from which it is made.

Clients want hard evidence of what their interior will look like, and to convince them thoroughly it is sensible to produce images that focus on materiality. This should be apparent in conventional perspectives, but often it is worth making additional images that give priority to finishes.

No traditional rendering method can rival the computer's capacity to represent materiality. Hand rendering relies on visual coding, of varying degrees of precision, to imply reality. Because such skills are highly specialist it was, and is, normal practice to employ a consultant 'visualizer' – who, through constant practice, can achieve something close to reality – to produce a handmade perspective. Such specialists inevitably have

Above and right
The computer deals objectively, as programmed, with the complexities of perspective, materiality and lighting within a precise three-dimensional representation of their context. These images illustrate particularly its capacity to plot and represent the interaction of reflective surfaces. Realistic and objective depiction eliminates the necessary stylization that was inevitable with hand rendering.

Above and left

More abstract evocations of transparent, translucent and opaque planes also demonstrate the computer's ability to calculate and emulate the surface qualities of different materials, their interactions and the impact of artificial and natural light sources.

Left
Relative levels of transparency are easy to control for flat glazed surfaces, but become more difficult when the glass is textured – or when, as here, soft fabrics hang loosely and in folds. It may be possible to scan examples of selected materials, but magnification of the original will result in distortion of scale. In this example, a suitable base texture was manipulated in the computer to represent folds and their transparency, along with varying levels of illumination.

Below
This image is concerned with the way glass, rising through an opening in the floor, responds to light from below. It demonstrates how the computer plots accurately the particular behaviour of light from a defined source on particular materials.

their own style, and designers tend to employ those whose technique they consider most compatible with the spirit of their project. The disadvantage is that, regardless of how attuned to each other designer and visualizer may be, the former is at the mercy of the latter, who will invitably not 'see' the proposal precisely as its creator intended. However, with regular practice and appropriate computer software, designers can now produce their own perspectives, expressing their vision exactly. Finishes, once the most difficult element of any drawing to make convincing, are now simple to represent and materials that would once have been presented as disjointed fragments on a sample board are now scanned with photographic accuracy and presented in context.

Existing finishes

This is an archetypical interior image, contained within a strict perimeter and with materials and colours meticulously rendered in order to give an accurate impression of the proposal. One particularly significant element within the interior is the fragment of existing plaster-ceiling moulding. It would be laborious to recreate this on computer, and the solution is to photograph it – preferably digitally, to allow the manipulation that will match the tonal values of the rendered image. When taking such a photograph it is important to position oneself as near as possible to the viewpoint of the intended rendering, so that the orientation and perspective of the existing feature is compatible with that of the virtual elements. Final adjustments can be made in the computer.

Left

It is often easier and more efficient to photograph existing finishes (such as the decorative plaster ceiling in this space) and scan them into computer illustrations, rather than trying to recreate them on a computer.

TIP PHOTOGRAPHING EXISTING MATERIALS

New construction, on the left of the image, complements the existing stone wall on the right. The existing wall was digitally photographed, scanned and manipulated. The problem of reconciling the perspective of the new drawing with that in a photograph is dealt with by the exaggeration of both, so that conventional rules are seen not to apply.

Below

In many projects with large areas of windows the view to the exterior is, necessarily, an integral part of the interior, and 'pasting' in a digital photograph of the street puts the proposal into context. The problem of incompatible perspective is likely to be significant, and again the solution is to distort the perspective of both elements. Additionally, the intensity of the street image is 'diluted' in order to suggest it being filtered through glass.

Opposite

This collage represents three major, and distinctly different, elements. The mundane, generic bookshelves – with their patchwork of book spines, scanned and pasted in with no attempt to refine them – transmute into outline, to match the representation of the existing masonry walls (depicted as a computer-made pastiche of a traditional architectural line drawing). The new stone floor with its irregular pattern is 'dropped in' at an inflated scale to make its grain visible. None of the three principle elements makes any attempt to conform to a common perspective, and thus they all avoid the problems of compatibility.

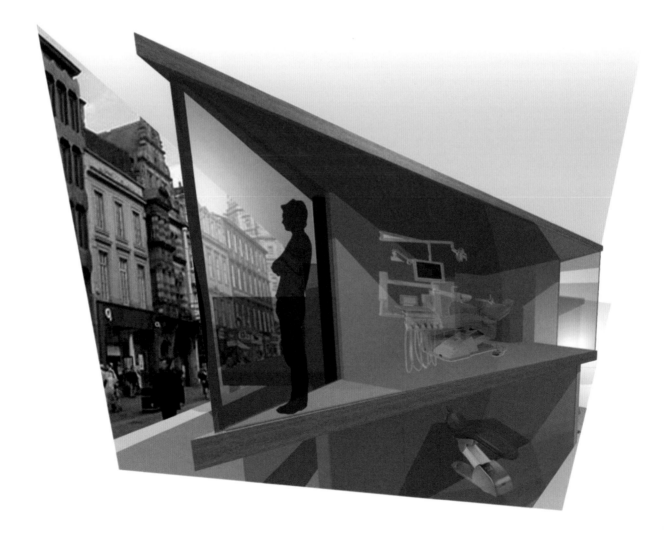

Left

Lighting effects are crucial to the success of this drawing and, by extension, to the proposed interior, which depends on a palette of dark, rich colours. The light, particularly that playing on the red wall and book 'tower', accentuates this richness. There is a subtle but crucial distinction in the quality of the natural light to the left of the red wall. The impact of the drawing also depends on the meticulous representation of detail, exemplified by the deep pile of the rug on the left-hand edge.

Furniture

Furniture is a fundamental component in any interior – the one element, in fact, with which users interact most directly – and it must be considered from the very beginning of the design process, because it helps to state the aesthetic theme of the interior.

Other than for one-off pieces, such as reception desks and bar counters, there is seldom a need to design furniture specifically for a project. A designer may enjoy isolated, inspired moments of creativity when a powerful idea springs tangentially from thinking about the entirety of a project and is worth pursuing, but these moments are rare and it is logical to select pieces instead from the superabundance of manufactured options. It could be argued that it demonstrates a lack of imagination or professional knowledge if one cannot find something suitable amongst the myriad variations of manufactured tables and chairs already available.

By and large, furniture conforms to strict size requirements and restrictions, and therefore familiar objects – such as chairs and tables – can be effective substitutes for the human figure in establishing the scale of an interior.

Above and right
This pair of images establishes a stylistic connection between the furniture and the interiors that contain it. The yellow-cube armchairs above reiterate the volume of the projecting floor above them. The charcoal 'blob' seats to the right match the colours and simplicity of their interior. The red units act as focal points.

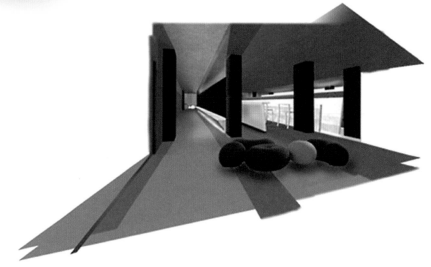

Above

Chairs and tables define this minimal response to a generously glazed corner site. A few pieces of crockery and cutlery, and a sleeping customer, provide diverting details.

Because furniture has such an impact on the character of an interior, it is important that it is accurately represented in any images. This may involve the resizing and pasting-in, by hand or computer, of photographs from catalogues and appropriate adjustment relative to the perspective of the space that accommodates them. It may mean the laborious creation of a near-likeness by hand or computer. Alternatively, and most efficiently and conveniently, it may mean the downloading, where it is available, of data from a manufacturer's website that will provide exact images of individual pieces, which may be convincingly manipulated and integrated within the constraints of an overall perspective.

Opposite and above
Two extraordinary pieces of
furniture are located wittily in
context. The detail in the drawings
seems to acknowledge their
singularity. In the opposite image,
the circular window and the face
it frames echo the inflated orange
tube and the figure within it. The
contorted faces on the screens in
the image above seem to despair
at the extraordinary seating that
floats beneath them.

TIP USING FURNITURE TO DEFINE A SPACE

Meticulous detailing and setting-out of
furniture, from data downloaded from a
manufacturer's website, gives reality to an
otherwise impressionistic rendering.

Downloading furniture from manufacturers' websites

There is little need for a designer to create new pieces of furniture for any but the most unique projects. Many manufacturers, to encourage selection of their own products, provide digital versions of pieces in their range which may be downloaded and used in plans, sections and, most spectacularly and usefully, in perspective views. Since furniture and fittings have such a fundamental importance in the expression of the character of an interior, it is important that they be rendered with precision. Downloading ensures this and eliminates the laborious creation of less accurate facsimiles.

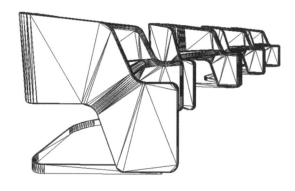

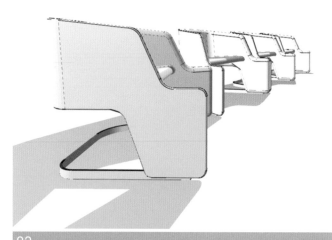

01
The data needed to construct a piece of furniture digitally is first downloaded as a wire-frame image, which allows the pieces to be precisely created compatible with the perspective of the intended finished image. It is in manufacturers' interests to supply this information free to encourage use of their products.

02
When the composition is acceptable, the elements may be made solid . . .

03
. . . and rendered with progressive refinement . . .

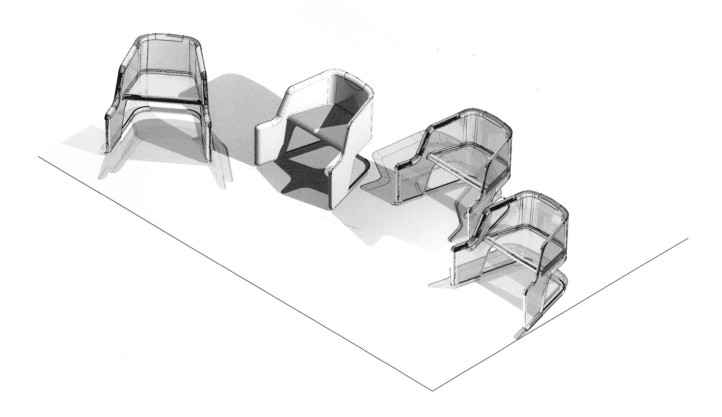

04
. . . the data may then be infinitely redeployed.

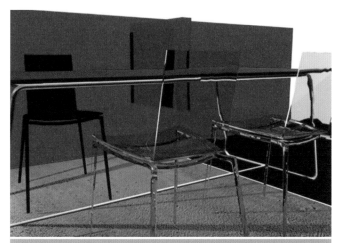

05
Such downloaded data is extremely refined and will create extraordinary, hyper-realistic images.

06
Specialist software persuasively represents the interaction of transparencies and reflectivities.

Figures

Human figures give scale to an interior and help explain how it will work and be inhabited, but photographs of completed interiors are notorious for being bereft of people. This makes some sense when making a photographic record of a pristine interior because changing fashions in clothes and haircuts can crudely date the most radical creation. Inappropriate dating is not a problem for presentation drawings, which need only be relevant to the time of their making and should be precisely of their time. The computer offers opportunities for including well-chosen figures that complement the aesthetic of the project. They can be witty or poetic, and may be particularly effective in engaging a client's imagination and sympathy.

It is notoriously difficult, in interior-design presentations, to incorporate lifelike drawings of people by hand. The body is too complex, and it is difficult to make the freehand lines of the drawing sit comfortably with the hard edges of the interior elements. It is therefore common practice to stylize the figure.

Left and above
Figures give scale to interior presentations but it is not necessary, and often impractical, for them to be highly detailed or lifelike – the use of stylized figures is common practice.

Left
These figures are traced outlines, made quickly to retain something of the spontaneity of a sketch. The use of outline allows the finishes to dominate the image.

Above
Figures can indicate changes of scale.

Right
Figures can clarify different levels and their use.

Far right
Transparent figures give scale without obscuring the interior.

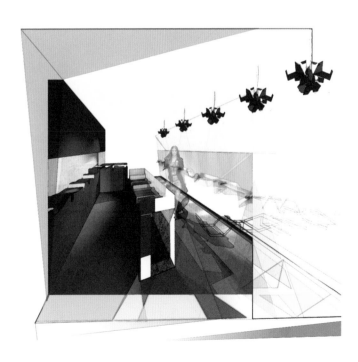

Such manipulation of the size and quality of an image is easier, and can be taken further, on computer. It is also possible to download, from free and subscription websites, batteries of figures in wide ranges of age, character and posture. There are sites that supply wholly digitally generated figures that may be programmed to adopt appropriate poses, but these are disturbingly characterless and unconvincing.

The most common practice is to build a personal library of figures from magazines, or to carry out project-specific searches for photographs of suitable 'characters' in appropriate positions. Generally, the figure should not dominate the interior but a well-chosen and adjusted figure can significantly influence perception of the design.

People obey the rules of perspective, and this is the major problem in including them in any drawing. Images can be culled from magazines, but they are often difficult to locate convincingly. (They may, for example, be at odds with the floor plane on which they are placed.) However, there are ways of dealing with this.

It is possible, for example, with a digital camera, to pose volunteers, or oneself, to meet project specific needs, and such digitally created images may be extensively manipulated within the computer for compatibility with the created image.

Left
Figures can look directly at viewers, inviting them into the interior or they can direct attention within the image.

Opposite
One way of ensuring that the figure is in sympathy with the perspective of its surroundings, and is adopting a pose appropriate to the designated activity of the space, is to create a bespoke image, easily done with digital photography.

Above
It is simple to record a series of slight variations, from which the most compatible may be chosen. Final, subtle adjustment on the computer should integrate the figure convincingly with the built elements. Here, the shadow – made freehand – suggests a convincing ground plane.

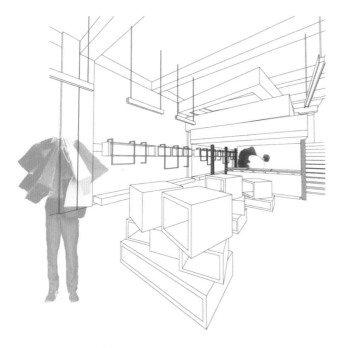

Above
The outline drawing clearly defines
three-dimensional forms and the
rendered version identifies finishes.

Composing the page

It is normal to put more than one image on each page of a presentation – if they all deal with the same area of the project. The order in which pages should be presented is usually self-evident – as is the issue of how images should be located on each sheet. The presentation constitutes the 'story' of the development of the project and, usually, it makes sense to start at the beginning and proceed logically to the end.

Images grouped together should complement each other. A perspective view might give an impression of atmosphere, but related plans and sections can contribute hard, practical information that will support and validate the aesthetic ambition of the project. While it is often important to provide physical samples of materials, it is also logical – and, with computers, increasingly easy – to scan in images of materials and artefacts that complement the drawn information. Scans of finishes should be located close to the areas to which they relate and repeated close to every area in which they appear. Comprehensive evidence, in image and text forms, eliminates the need for superfluous embellishments. Lines around, or lines linking, images are more likely to confuse than to clarify, and an elaborate and repetitive titling of each sheet is pointless and visually redundant. It may, however, be diplomatic to feature a client's corporate identity.

For most projects, there is no need to make big drawings. A3, often A4, sized drawings will support as much information as a client might be expected to assimilate without the punctuation of regular page turning. It is easier to discuss smaller sheets than large boards around a table, and much easier to carry them through the streets on the way to a presentation. It is also likely that an image, or collection of images, which work at A3 for a group presentation will also be legible in A4 format if left for individual perusal after the meeting.

Each page needs to be composed. When images are organized methodically they tend to end up on a regular grid, which makes it difficult to establish meaningful connections or to get a balance of size and visual weight. A better rule of thumb is to identify the key image for each sheet, to locate that centrally – or just above or below the centre – and place supporting images around it, aiming to establish a balance by the manipulation of their relative sizes and distance from the central image.

Below

The fragment of inset plan identifies the location within the project of the dominant three-dimensional image, which is complemented by information about the finishes of existing and new walls. The different component images combine to make a single, coherent sheet of drawings.

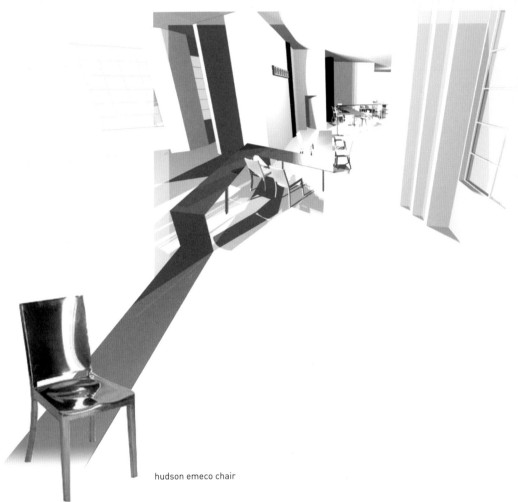

hudson emeco chair

view of ground floor looking up to study area

section A–A of ground floor showing office walls scale 1:200

This ground-floor plan and axonometric describe the proposal in factual terms. The plan demonstrates layout and provides a key. The axonometric extrudes the ground floor and relates it spatially to the upper level and moulded ceiling.

The three-dimensional view that dominates this sheet explains, in a deliberately selective and mannered fashion, the configuration of the major elements. However, its main function is to establish the atmosphere created by materials and lighting – and this is complemented by the scanned images of materials and fittings, set out formally and objectively.

Right
The spatial arrangement of the proposal is explained factually using a ground-floor plan and axonometric diagram.

Opposite
The three-dimensional perspective and accompanying presentation sheet illustrate the atmosphere, lighting and specific materials and furnishings to be used.

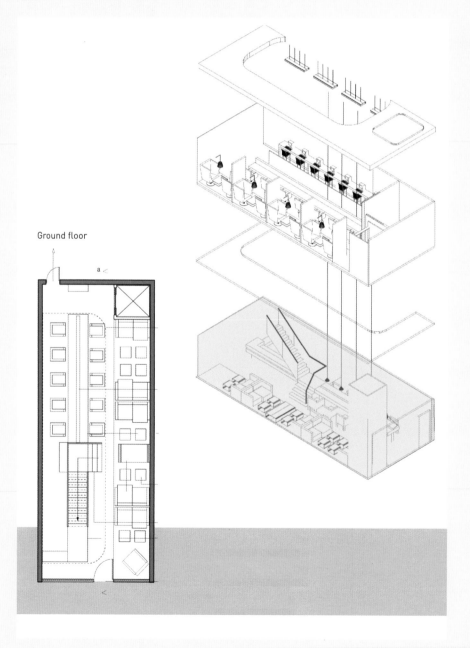

Ground floor

Seating area and stairs to the first floor

Darker colour schemes and concealed atmospheric lighting gives this area a more relaxed mood. There is a deliberate continuity between the staircase, bar and work surface, expressing the flexibility of the space.

1   2   3   4   5   6   7

1. pendant chandelier
2. American walnut veneer
3. ionized steel
4. quartz flooring
5. steel
6. red poppy fabric
7. black resin flooring

Explaining things

It is always good practice to begin a presentation by explaining the ideas, whether about organization or ambience, which underpin a project, so that the rationale for subsequent steps is clear and convincing. Such drawings tend to be most effective when they are simple, and although simple images can be bland, the computer's capacity to represent colour and texture can create dynamic diagrams out of them.

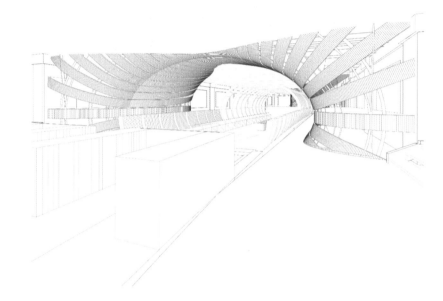

Top
The abstracted 'winged' image on the left expresses the spirit of the tensile structure in situ on the right.

Above
An evocation of the effects of artificial lighting on reflective surfaces.

Right
A computer-generated structure superimposed on a digital photograph.

TIP CLARIFYING COMPLICATED ELEMENTS

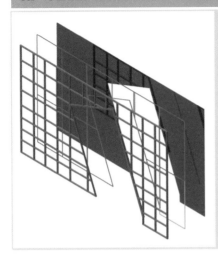

The reduction of complicated or unfamiliar elements to their constituent parts can help in the understanding of the whole. Here, the separation of layers around a skewed wall opening gives clarification.

Above
An expression of essential elements.

Linear and tonal clarity

The computer is an ideal tool for representing materiality. Most projects deal with modest rectangular single-storey spaces and therefore an accurate depiction of surfaces and finishes is all that is needed to explain the nature of the design proposal. There are, however, other projects when the character of an internal space is defined more usefully by the representation of more complex three-dimensional conditions and gestures. The clarity of these is often lost in elaborately rendered images that obscure the clear expression of form and depth. Information about complex volumes is more effectively conveyed in line drawings that strategically use the minimum of hue and tone, and then only where they help to clarify the expression of solidity.

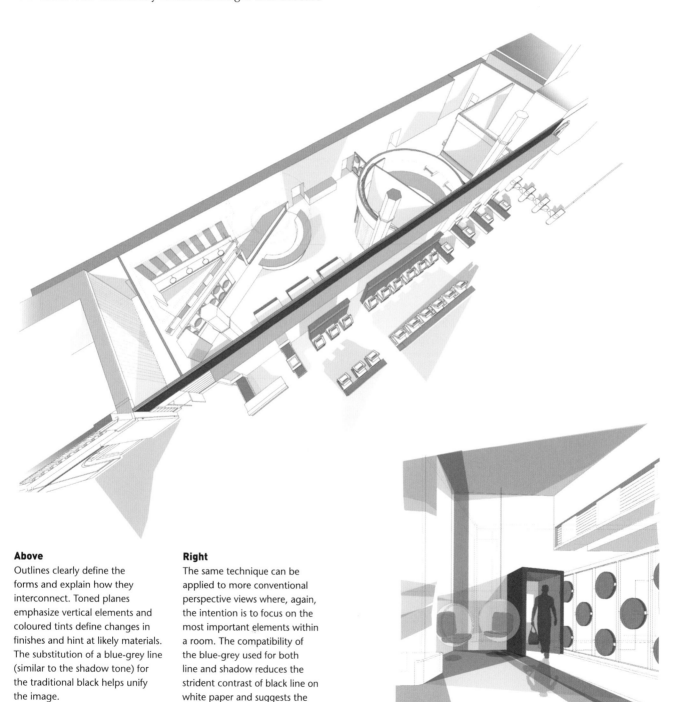

Above
Outlines clearly define the forms and explain how they interconnect. Toned planes emphasize vertical elements and coloured tints define changes in finishes and hint at likely materials. The substitution of a blue-grey line (similar to the shadow tone) for the traditional black helps unify the image.

Right
The same technique can be applied to more conventional perspective views where, again, the intention is to focus on the most important elements within a room. The compatibility of the blue-grey used for both line and shadow reduces the strident contrast of black line on white paper and suggests the transparency of the space.

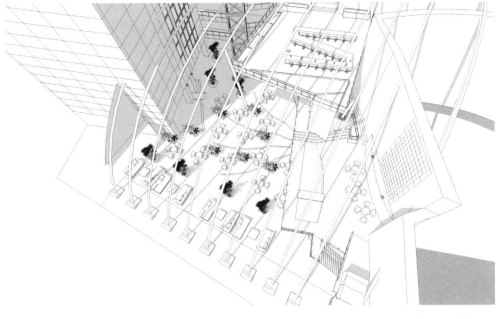

Left

Dramatic perspective drawing underlines the height of this internal volume and is emphasized by the lines of joints in the wall claddings. The single flat shadow tone is enough to give three-dimensional solidity. The recognizable elements of furniture and plants give scale.

Below left

In this more conventional view of the same space the block of shadow is enough to convey the suspension of the foreground level, which would inevitably be less apparent in the complexity of a fully rendered view. Again, furniture and plants give scale and explain how the areas will be used.

Right

The formal simplicity of this image explains the symmetrical organization of the interior. Removing the roof, perhaps perversely, draws attention to the gable that establishes the characteristic symmetry of the existing building. Flat tones on receding walls emphasize the cross walls and gable.

Case stud   s

Left

A digital collage of shapes, colours, textures and artefacts creates an impression. Found objects and materials, such as the mounted goat's head and back wall, are scanned and pasted, while others, such as the curved foreground elements, are quickly generated on computer.

Opposite

The image on the right aims to give an impression of how a comparatively small space will be transformed by complex veneers of colours, images and artefacts. The 'wire frame' lines suggest the existing walls. Such an image can whet a client's appetite for an extraordinary possibility, and while it has all the apparent creative energy of an uninhibited rendering made in conventional media, it is much closer to being an achievable conclusion. Surfaces, like the wall on the left and the image of the red haired head, can be exactly reproduced and converted into viable building materials by digital printing on paper, cloth, wood, metal or plastic. In the image on the left a diagrammatic view explains the location of elements.

Ultimately the success of an interior depends on the expression of its surfaces and their materiality and of the objects, furniture, light fittings and artefacts that the interior contains. A good designer orchestrates the interaction of these elements to create the harmony of the whole.

At an early stage in a project's evolution it is often more important to evoke the anticipated atmosphere, rather than the technical details, so that it may be tested and communicated to a client for approval. It is therefore appropriate to make images that concentrate on materials and artefacts rather than the precise delineation of the space. In the real interior the user's eye and imagination will engage with these details, particularly in the

modest rectangular spaces that constitute most interiors.

The computer's capacity to scan materials, textures and form precisely allows their accurate representation, to a scale and in a relationship that is superior even to the sample board, on which these elements can be collected together but on which their relative sizes cannot be conveyed.

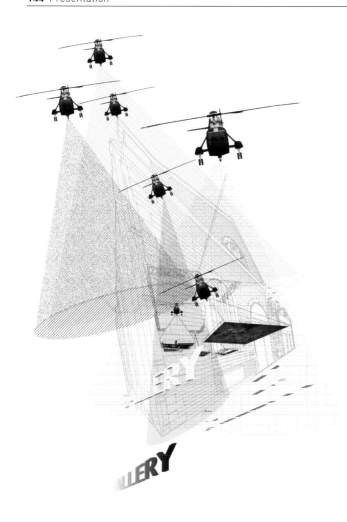

Text

While most presentations are made face-to-face with clients, with verbal explanations to support the images, it is still important to become adept at adding text to visual material. This is emphatically not about writing a long, supporting essay. Ideas should be defined with a minimum of evocative words – using well-crafted phrases rather than sentences, and words rather than phrases. It is productive to explain the evolution of ideas so that clients understand the rationale underpinning the final outcome. Clients usually have their own expectations of a project, and if these are not met they need to be persuaded that the alternative is the consequence of serious analytical thinking.

Before the advent of computers, and except for a small minority of designers with impeccable handwriting, applying text was a time-consuming process that involved stencils or rub-on transfer lettering. Consequently, written information tended to be strictly factual, confined to the identification of floor levels and the naming of rooms. Now it is as simple to add words as it is to draw lines, and while this may encourage verbal excess it also offers the potential to make drawings more accessible.

Before computers, text tended to be black on white. Now options exist for infinite colours and shades of grey. These present fascinating possibilities but demand editing, not only to keep text brief but also to create hierarchies of information. The most important information should be visually assertive.

Above
Letters may be shaped and toned to respond to the composition of the image.

Right
The line of text is appropriately distorted and connects the two versions of the same drawing, of which the 'de-saturated', lower version acts as a backdrop for the more significant text that names the project with a more assertive font.

Opposite
Text explains the conceptual intention.

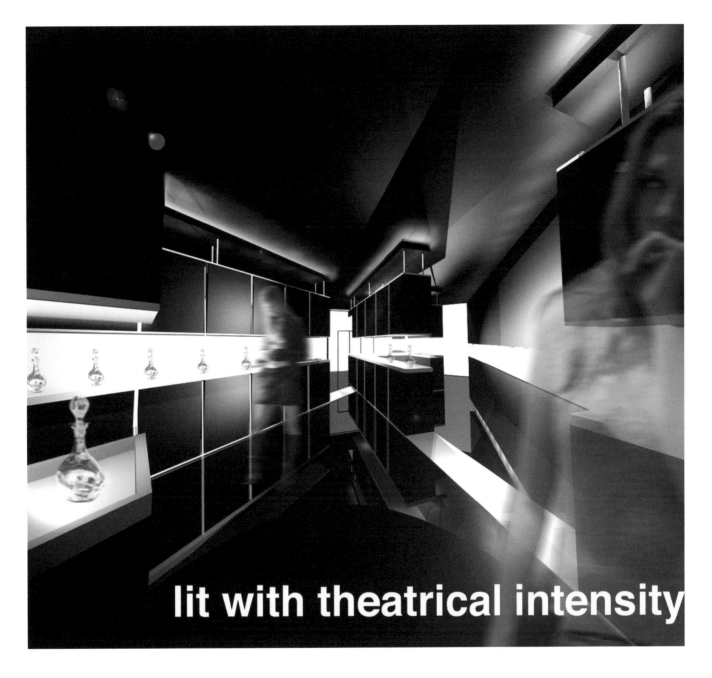

lit with theatrical intensity

Size and colour of letter may be adjusted. Fonts may be changed. Styles may be varied.

Successful text should, however, be an integral part of a drawing and compatible with the style of the interior proposed. It needs careful consideration in order to ensure that the whole does not deteriorate into visual cacophony.

Remember that most clients will feel comfortable with words and more confident about criticizing them than about questioning the content of drawings. Crude grammar and inept spelling will inevitably undermine credibility. Always use spell and grammar checks, then read the text again to be quite sure it is convincing.

It is generally good to leave presentation material behind after a meeting for a client to mull over, and text will prompt recollection of verbal explanation and focus attention on the essential messages. Extravagant, speculative claims should be avoided. They may goad a sceptical client into dissent.

Text may be used in any drawing – including perspective views, in which it can add a brief and useful commentary and suggest an invisible vertical plane that accentuates the receding perspective.

Above and below
A meticulously detailed model
can provide the most convincing
explanation of how areas
interrelate and how complex
plan-forms develop.

Model-making

Computers create virtual models: astonishingly accurate, three-dimensional representations of interiors that may be rotated in virtual space and viewed from whichever angle the designer chooses – either to inform the creative process or to communicate ideas to clients and colleagues. Such images are convincing – up to a point. However, whether on screen or on paper, they lack a sense of spatial volume. They remain essentially two-dimensional and, while the eye and mind can respond to the implication of depth and space, the 'real' distance between planes is not tangible. Convincing perception of spatial depth is infallibly conveyed in the simplest real (as opposed to virtual) models, regardless of their scale. The physical model does not require any interpretation of two-dimensional evidence by eye and mind, which do not appear to have difficulty coping with the most extreme reductions in scale.

The model's capacity for simple, direct spatial communication overcomes the problems, and anxieties, that the majority of non-professionals experience when confronted with two and three-dimensional drawings. In addition, everyone appears to enjoy the results of miniaturization and the game of imaging how they would inhabit the space thus described.

The physical model is particularly valuable in presentations to a group of clients, where it is always difficult to know to what extent individuals within the group may understand drawings. However, it is reasonable to be confident that they will all make an accurate interpretation of a model and, consequently, be less reticent about asking questions or commenting.

Just as it is impossible to do full justice in a drawing to the volumetric reality of a space, so it is impossible to convey in photographs the 'real' model's capacity to represent that space convincingly. Nevertheless, it is worth showing a couple of examples (see following pages).

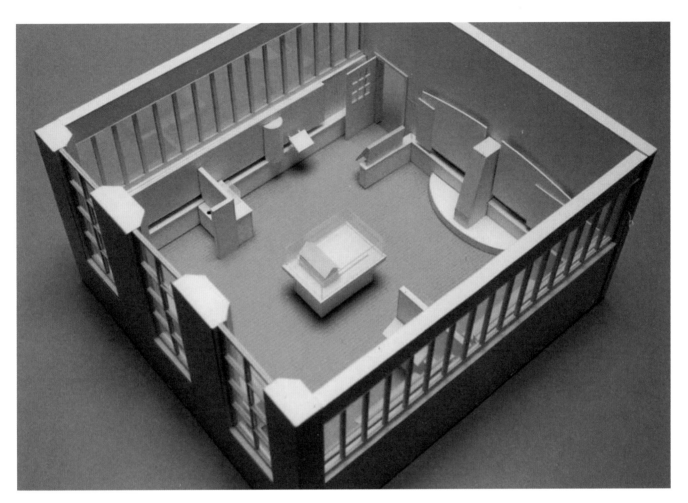

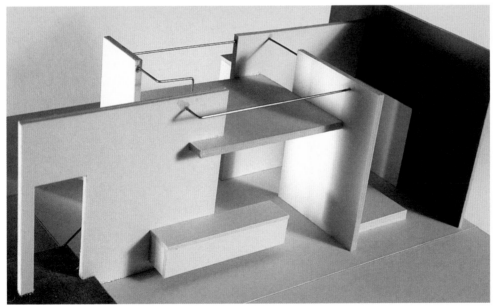

Above

A highly finished model (scale 1:50) to explain an exhibition project to a client committee. All the walls are modelled because they have a significant presence, and the proposed objects are modestly scaled and isolated within a 'room' that is big enough to be peered into. The model of the model building in the central perspex display cabinet is an example of the whimsical miniaturization that can fascinate and charm clients.

Left

Sometimes, particularly when explaining a complex plan, it is more sensible to model only the most significant or relevant elements in a proposal. Here, the black plane represents the existing wall, and new walls are white. The comparatively slight handrail is included because of its crucial aesthetic role.

Model-making tools

Models, like drawings, may be divided into those that are dedicated to the process of developing a design and those that are set pieces, made for presentation to a client. Both require very simple, comparatively cheap, materials and equipment, but need continuous practice to develop and sustain their quality.

The convention is that models should be white – to maximize the effects of light and shade. Colour and representation of materials is best left to computer-generated images. It is possible, however, to achieve a convincing representation of finishes and fittings when the scale is increased to 1:20 or 1:10.

Clear plastic sheet can represent glass, and if scoured with a fine sandpaper makes convincing frosted glass.

Balsa wood is easy to cut and represents timber surfaces well (although the grain can appear out of scale).

Indented plastic can represent tiled floors and walls. If coloured with a thin paint, the grid will remain visible.

These materials may be obtained from specialist model-making suppliers.

Models that are produced to help the design process,

01
The most useful sheet material is thin, white cardboard or plastic sheet. The first is easy to cut, and at 3 or 6 millimetre (around ¼ inch) thicknesses accurately represents internal walls at 1:100 and 1:50 scales respectively. Plastic sheet bends more easily to approximate curved forms, and is stronger.

02
A ruler and pencil will mark out sizes and shapes. A metal ruler also provides a straight cutting edge: a flat ruler will do, but the type with a triangular profile is easier to hold firmly in place. A robust scalpel, with frequently replaced blades, will make a clean cut.

03
For a clean cut, the side of the scalpel blade should make a right angle with the sheet. The ruler should be pressed very firmly to prevent its slipping. The green rubber cutting mat protects table surfaces.

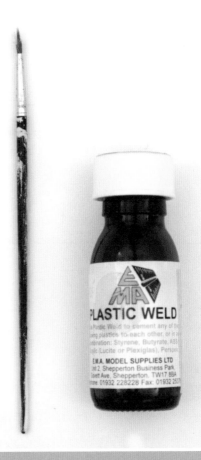

04

Different adhesives are necessary for different materials: that on the left, for cardboard and wood; that in the centre, for gluing flat surfaces together; that on the right will stick anything, but is particularly useful for instant spot-fixing of columns and figures.

05

Liquid plastic glue and a brush are used for joining edges.

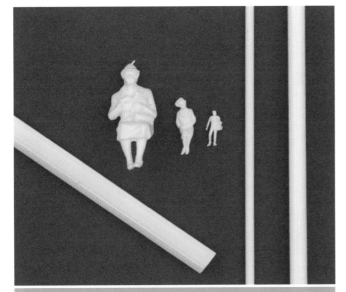

06

Model-making suppliers also provide plastic figures to appropriate scales – here 1:50, 1:100 and 1:200. They also offer various columns and generic furniture pieces.

07

Once the required piece is cut, liquid plastic glue is most effectively applied using a brush.

like exploratory sketches, should not be too carefully made. Like drawn sketches, they should be taken only as far as is necessary for them to deliver their information. They should be to any convenient scale, but if this is small enough, walls and floors can be made from thick paper, which is easy to cut accurately with scalpel or scissors. Quickly made models, like paper sketches, may be thrown away or pulled apart and reconfigured without regret but, like a good sketch on paper, may also be tidied up and used in a preliminary presentation to client or colleagues.

When a more formal presentation is required, then the model can be produced with exacting precision and finished to eliminate the rough junctions and other imperfections from the developmental stage. The basic construction is the same and, at the end, the whole is spray-painted to eliminate fingermarks and tonal variations between different materials.

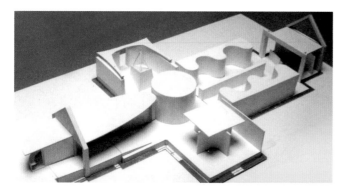

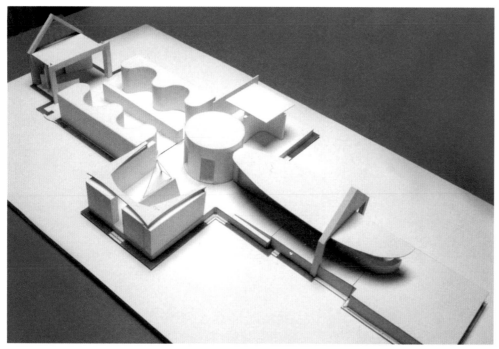

Above left and left
Two photographs of a model for a more formal presentation. Rough junctions and imperfections have been finished and smoothed over, and the whole has been spray painted white to cover dirty marks and variations on material.

Above and left

This example, at 1:50 scale and no bigger than 120 mm x 70 mm (5 x 3 inches), demonstrates that the smallest model can be finished with extraordinary detail. Two walls define the existing volume, and the profile of the right-hand side is determined by the plan of the missing wall. The figures establish an accurate perception of the size of the space. The computer-generated image of the same space (left), deals with colours and materials. It does not need to be as explicit about three-dimensional form.

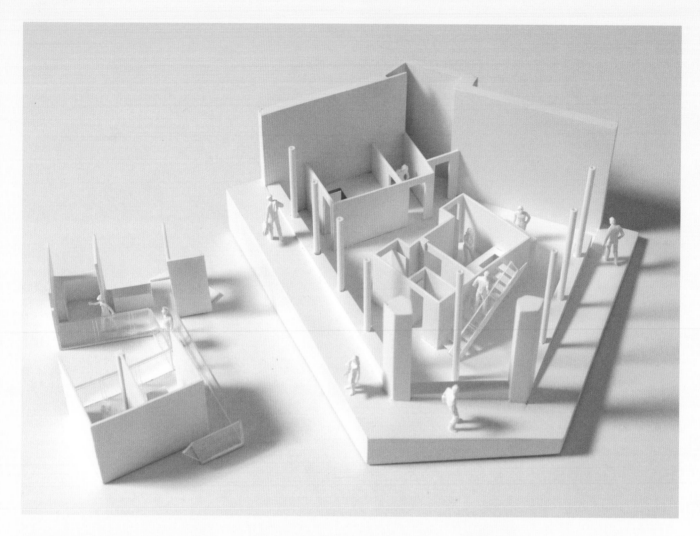

With complex interiors on more than one floor, it is often sensible to make a model that may be demounted to reveal different levels. In this example, the piece on the left sits on top of the elements in the middle of the plan. Its removal reveals how seating is tucked under the upper level in the central space, and how the balcony covers the desk on the upper right.

The 1:20 detail above shows the recessed seating in the central space on the ground floor of the previous model.

At this scale, furniture may be accurately represented and battery-powered miniature light fittings added. The wood grain of the door, the sheen of the floor tiles and the recessed skirting detail are persuasive – as is the wall colour. Painting models is difficult because the paints used often have a reflectivity that reacts unconvincingly to light. The secret is to use the same emulsion paint as would be used on the real walls, bought in small 'tester pots' and slightly diluted to suit the scale of the model. This 'real' paint finish accounts for the naturalistic play of light on the recessed wall.

Just as digital technology has transformed the making of drawings for interior design, so it is beginning to have an impact on the making of models. Digital information produced in the development of plans and sections can now be used to programme laser cutting and rapid prototyping equipment to create models of extreme precision, at any scale. The accuracy of the finished product, together with the need for detailed programming of the machinery, means that the process is most suitable for final presentation models and, given the very high cost of detailed handmade models, is already an attractive alternative to the traditionally crafted variety. Just as the initial handmade sketch drawing remains the preferred tool for early design work, so the handmade sketch model is liable to remain the preferred method of three-dimensional exploration. However, just as we are beginning to see designers who are computer literate use the keyboard as a 'sketching' tool (pages 82–83) so we are likely to see the development of new three-dimensional modelling programmes which will allow more casual exploitation of the potential.

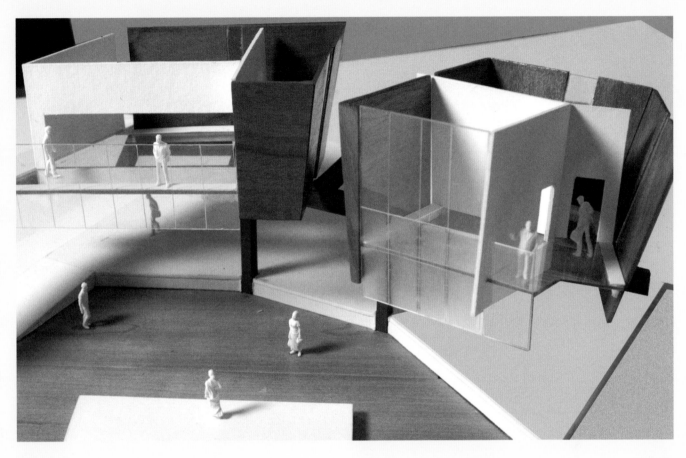

Opposite
When explaining multi-level spaces, it is often helpful to present a model that may be demounted to reveal different levels.

Above
It is not always necessary to model every part of an interior. This model concentrates on two mezzanine areas, explaining how they are supported and interconnect. Accurate but diagrammatic representation of four crucial materials further clarifies the composition.

Right
The computer has begun to make inroads into physical model-making and is particularly useful for producing rounded forms. In this example a rapid-prototyping maching makes complex shapes using the information already set out in computer-generated plans and sections.

Chapter 4
Production

The designer's role

After formal presentation, and once the client has approved the final design drawings, it is the designer's job to produce a set of 'working drawings' or 'production drawings'. The number of these will vary from project to project, but their function remains the same. They will provide the building contractor, and anyone else involved in the construction process, with a comprehensive description in drawings and words of the full extent and quality of the work necessary to complete the project satisfactorily. They will also act as a formal record of the details of the contractual agreement between client and builders.

The designer must not only provide plans and sections of the complete project but of every element within that project, in order to describe in detail the materials to be used, the sizes of components and the method for their assembly.

Right and below
These drawings show how essential information about one, comparatively simple, element is communicated to a contractor.

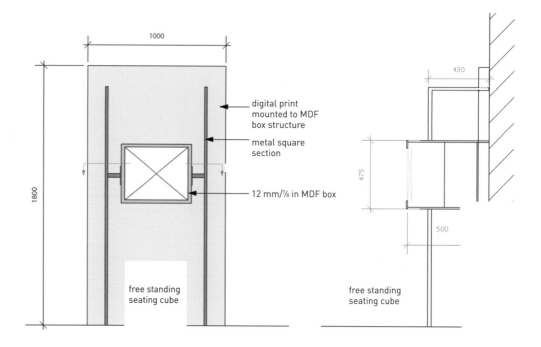

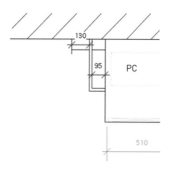

1:20-scaled drawings set out dimensions and describe materials.

Tone, colour and three-dimensional images make the drawings more comprehensible.

1:5-scaled drawing allows room for the detailed notes necessary to describe the most complex areas. The scale is further increased to 1:1 (full size) when necessary, and tone and colour again increase clarity.

It is desirable that a designer also takes responsibility for the supervision of work on site if quality is to be assured and the unforeseen difficulties that often come to light during construction are to be dealt with successfully.

When difficulties or disputes arise it is also the designer's role to act as an 'arbitrator' to ensure, on the client's behalf, that the extent and quality of the job matches that quoted for; and, on the contractor's behalf, that payment is made for completed work and for extra, unforeseen work that may have become necessary during the course of the contract. Sometimes such problems are the result of site conditions that were not apparent during the initial surveys, which may have been done before it was possible to carry out exploratory demolition. Sometimes they may result from changing requirements on the client's side. Occasionally, they are the result of the designer's error, and, although it may be painful to admit this, it is usually sensible to do so since it will be fairly obvious who is to blame, and stubbornly maintaining innocence in the face of contradictory evidence can only lead to a loss of credibility and trust.

The completed set of production drawings will allow a builder to estimate the cost of the building work and produce a 'tender', which is an estimated cost of all necessary work, including labour and materials. It is the total sum for which the builder is prepared to carry out all the work. Sometimes clients will nominate a contractor, usually on the basis of a previous successful collaboration, and it will then be the designer's job to advise on the fairness of the uncontested tender.

It is, however, more usual for at least three contractors to tender for a job, and for the one offering the lowest price to be given the work. It then becomes the designer's responsibility to check that the successful contractor is capable of carrying out the work to a satisfactory standard. This applies particularly if the tender is lower than anticipated, which can suggest that the contractor has miscalculated or is over-anxious to get the work and may not have the reserve resources to deal adequately with complications that might arise in the course of the contract.

It is often difficult to estimate the cost of an interior project accurately. When operating in new buildings the nature of the work may be clearly defined and estimated, and it is very unlikely that unanticipated work or

TIP THREE DIMENSIONS CLARIFY TWO

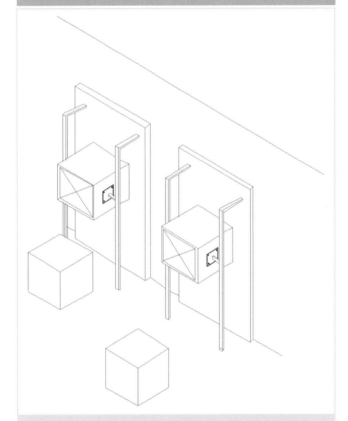

While dimensions and construction information are most effectively conveyed in two-dimensional drawings, it will often help a contractor understand how they come together if the intended three-dimensional outcome is also shown. The computer makes the generation of this image from the two-dimensional data very simple.

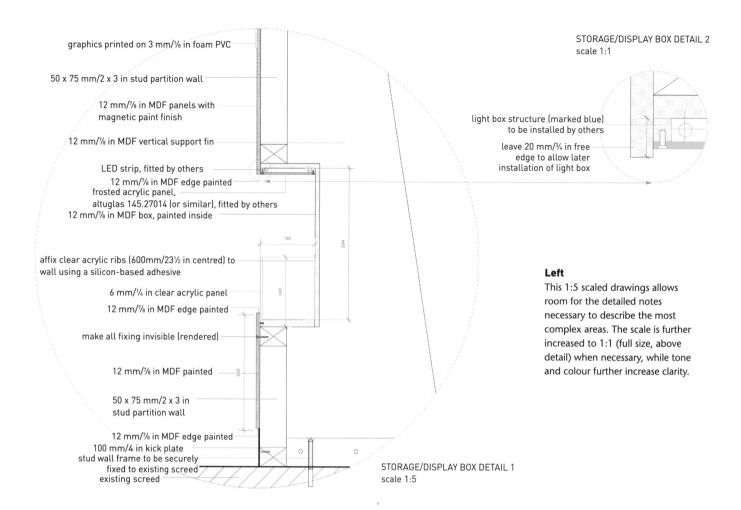

graphics printed on 3 mm/⅛ in foam PVC

50 x 75 mm/2 x 3 in stud partition wall

12 mm/⅞ in MDF panels with magnetic paint finish

12 mm/⅞ in MDF vertical support fin

LED strip, fitted by others

12 mm/⅞ in MDF edge painted
frosted acrylic panel,
altuglas 145.27014 (or similar), fitted by others
12 mm/⅞ in MDF box, painted inside

affix clear acrylic ribs (600mm/23½ in centred) to wall using a silicon-based adhesive

6 mm/¼ in clear acrylic panel

12 mm/⅞ in MDF edge painted

make all fixing invisible (rendered)

12 mm/⅞ in MDF painted

50 x 75 mm/2 x 3 in stud partition wall

12 mm/⅞ in MDF edge painted
100 mm/4 in kick plate
stud wall frame to be securely
fixed to existing screed
existing screed

STORAGE/DISPLAY BOX DETAIL 2
scale 1:1

light box structure (marked blue) to be installed by others

leave 20 mm/¾ in free edge to allow later installation of light box

STORAGE/DISPLAY BOX DETAIL 1
scale 1:5

Left
This 1:5 scaled drawings allows room for the detailed notes necessary to describe the most complex areas. The scale is further increased to 1:1 (full size, above detail) when necessary, while tone and colour further increase clarity.

significant amendments to the first contract will occur. With work to existing buildings, cost estimation is more difficult. Complications are often unforeseeable, and emerge in the course of the work as existing finishes are stripped back and structural problems are exposed.

It is also in the nature of interiors projects that the finishes and construction details that make up the bulk of the work will be unique to the particular scheme, and therefore an accurate price depends on the contractors' perception of the intrinsic difficulties involved in meeting unfamiliar demands. Contractors inevitably prefer to work with familiar materials and techniques and, if they have the option of an easier job, will submit an expensive quote for complicated work to ensure that undertaking difficult work will be rewarded and unforeseen costs will be covered. The simple, familiar project will almost always prove cheaper. A project that strays from the familiar will also require extra commitment from a client, who may be inspired to agree to an expensive option by a seductive presentation but whose initial enthusiasm will weaken if there are a succession of expensive, unanticipated or unacknowledged complications. It is normal, and logical, that the designer will be blamed for practical inefficiencies and overspending if creative

ambition contributes to difficulties. A designer persuading a client to commit to an ambitious or innovative project must be prepared to spend more time detailing and supervising its construction, quite probably for the same fee as a more conventional solution.

Clients always have a budget beyond which they cannot or will not go. While they often have some capacity to extend this, there is usually a point at which it becomes apparent that it will be necessary to negotiate details of the work with the contractor in order to reduce the overall cost. The designer is crucial to this process because decisions must be made about how savings will least prejudice the aesthetic and practical efficiency of the finished work, and only the designer has the overview and knowledge to resolve such compromises successfully.

Production drawings

There is no room for ambiguity in production drawings. They should be clear and, as far as possible, simple. Even for the most complicated project, simple drawings will usually signify well-resolved thinking and an economical and effective solution, easily built and robust. It is important to appreciate that, while drawings are produced in a comfortable studio environment with instruments designed to maximize accuracy, they will be interpreted and implemented in the confusion of a building site. They should therefore be as easy to understand as possible. Workers on site are not necessarily familiar with the potential of the materials specified and the techniques required to use them.

All project information can be distributed digitally, and this cuts out the delays and uncertainties that were previously an inevitable aspect of postal delivery. The advantages are obvious, in that delays that affect the price or completion times can be diminished. The disadvantage is that the designer is under greater pressure to respond quickly to unforeseen complications and, given that such revisions can have a significant and not immediately apparent impact on the whole project and its cost, it is sensible to agree a reasonable amount of time for consideration of each development. If a designer has given evidence of general efficiency, been sympathetic to the contractor's problems and is confronting an unforeseeable dilemma, then it is reasonable to expect understanding in return.

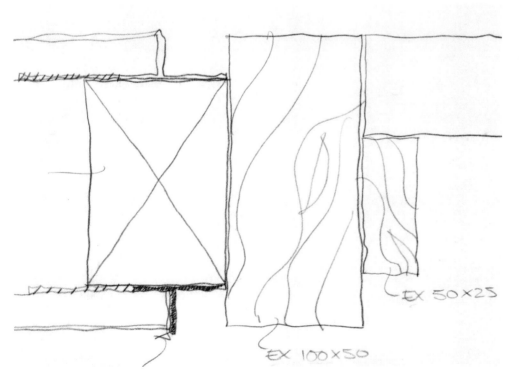

Left
Being able to draw a fast freehand detail – this example for a door jamb is roughly scaled – remains a useful skill when discussing options with colleagues or giving instructions on site.

The conventions

There are two distinct categories of production drawing:
plans and sections, which are likely to be at 1:50 or 1:100
scale, and perhaps at 1:20 for small projects; and details,
which explain the construction of typical elements or
which isolate and explain complex conditions. Details
are likely to be drawn at 1:5 or 1:10, and sometimes full
size or half full size – although the latter is considered
potentially misleading because it is easy to confuse half
with full size, and the misinterpreted drawing can then
imply a more elegant solution than will achieved in
reality.

While it is desirable that the nature of production
drawings evolves in response to the improved capacities
of the computer, respect for established drawing
conventions is essential. A shared visual language is vital
if the complexity of construction information is to be
communicated unambiguously to contractors and other
building-industry professionals.

Once again, graphic conventions have been partly
evolved in response to the materials available for making
them. When drawings were almost exclusively made
with ink or pencil line on tracing paper, for reproduction
by dye-line and photocopying, the articulation of

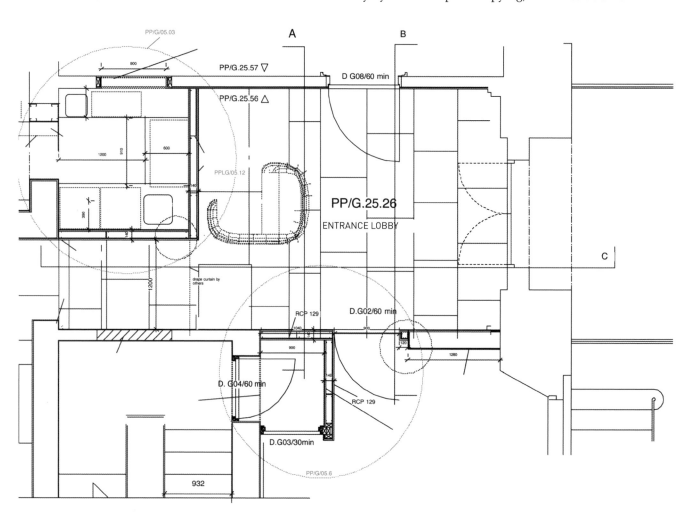

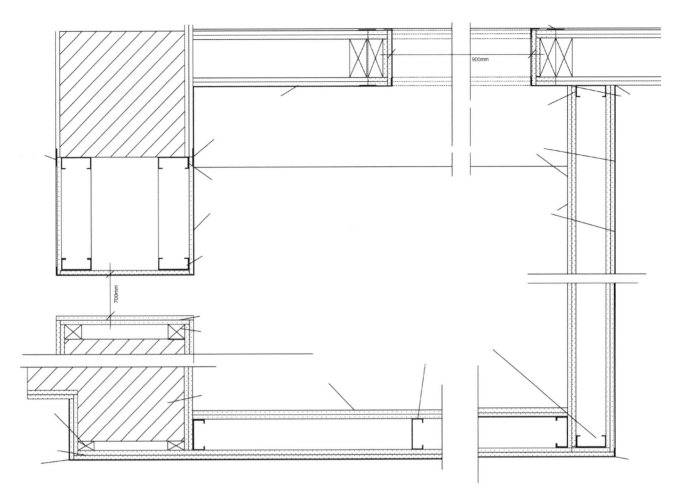

components within the drawing was achieved by varying line thicknesses, hatchings and cross-hatchings. This process was time-consuming and, because the drawings were made in conformity with strictly established codes, it was viable and common practice to employ specialist technicians and 'tracers' to draft the volume of drawings necessary for the more substantial projects. These assistants tended to have responsibility for evolving and finalizing work initiated by the designers who led the team. They did not take responsibility for final decision-making, but often had valuable practical knowledge: the result of sustained involvement with technical detailing.

The switch to computer production reduced the need for repetitive hand drawing, and consequently the number of individuals engaged in the compilation of production information. The content of such drawings, however, has not changed much. Variations are small, but they have significantly changed the look of the final drawing. Lines, because specified into the computer rather than plotted by hand, are wholly precise. Quality of reproduction is standardized and perfect. Mistakes are now intellectual rather than manual.

Above
Complex plan areas are drawn at 1:10 in order to create room for the detailed drawing and extensive notes necessary to provide comprehensive instructions.

Detail drawings

Often the first proposal for a construction detail,
particularly if it uses familiar materials in a familiar
context, will adhere closely to initial expectations.
However, unanticipated problems constantly emerge
because the precise characteristics of each project are
different, and aspects of the solution to one problem can
very often have an impact on the resolution of apparently
unrelated details.

All detail drawings, like all other design drawings,
begin with a designer's first thoughts, and, like them, are
likely to be scribbled in a notebook or sketch pad. The
process for developing them is also essentially the same.
After initial, informed but unstructured thinking, the
defining move must be made to scaled drawing in order
to test ideas rigorously before producing the final version,
and to ensure an accurate perception of the relative
sizes of individual elements and their exact relationship
one to another. From such beginnings the complexity
of thinking grows, as the interaction of materials and
construction comes under sustained scrutiny.

While details must always be considered in three
dimensions, it is standard practice to draw options

and present conclusions in two, as plans and sections. This isolates and simplifies particular aspects of the problem and its solution, and so helps clarify thinking. It also presents information to the builder or maker in a more comprehensible form. It may be useful to add three-dimensional projections in order to clarify how parts relate, but unless the forms are very simple it is generally difficult to read dimensions and notes against three-dimensional images. The computer generates three-dimensional views much more quickly and efficiently than the hand, and those produced for earlier presentation work may be easily transferred to production documents in order to clarify the intended outcome.

There is perhaps an instinct amongst traditionally trained designers that is suspicious of the introduction of more accessible, superficially frivolous drawings during the production phase. However, if it is accepted that drawings made for a client should be as accessible as possible then the same should be true of drawings created for use on site. It was the difficulties of adding colour, tone and a third dimension (because of the drawing instruments and reproduction equipment available) that, until recently, have excluded them from the repertoire

Above
First thoughts about details, committed to a notebook following a discussion on site (left) and then in a sketch pad in the studio (right).

Below and bottom

These two drawings specify materials and dimensions and give construction information. The small plan at the left of the bottom drawing provides information about the location and application of the more detailed information in the section. The figures, again, immediately establish scale, and (perhaps) lighten the contractors' task and amuse the designer in the midst of otherwise serious work.

of production drawings. The computer makes their inclusion simple and their blanket exclusion foolish.

It is obviously worth taking advantage of the advances and variations that the computer makes possible. Tones can effectively replace hatchings, which can be visually strident. Various coloured lines may be used because they are as easy to reproduce as a black line. However, it is important that the potential for variations is treated intelligently. Too much will result in incoherence. Differences in line thicknesses and tones must be readily distinguishable to the eye if they are to contribute to clarity.

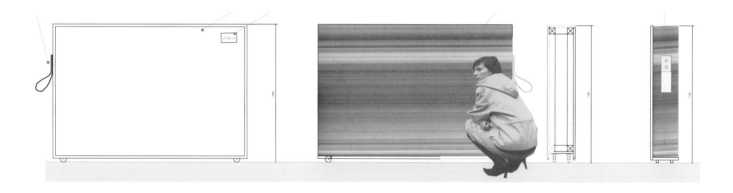

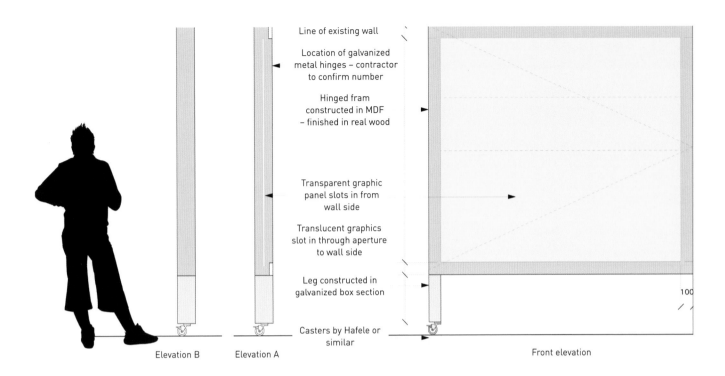

Line of existing wall

Location of galvanized
metal hinges – contractor
to confirm number

Hinged fram
constructed in MDF
– finished in real wood

Transparent graphic
panel slots in from
wall side

Translucent graphics
slot in through aperture
to wall side

Leg constructed in
galvanized box section

Casters by Hafele or
similar

Elevation B   Elevation A

Front elevation

100

Section through room 1:100

Plan

Above

In this example, pale tints colour-code the drawings and ease the identification of materials. Simple, silhouetted figures immediately establish scale, making the drawing instantly accessible. The drawings specify materials and give construction information, while the small plan at the bottom provides information about the application of the more detailed information in the section.

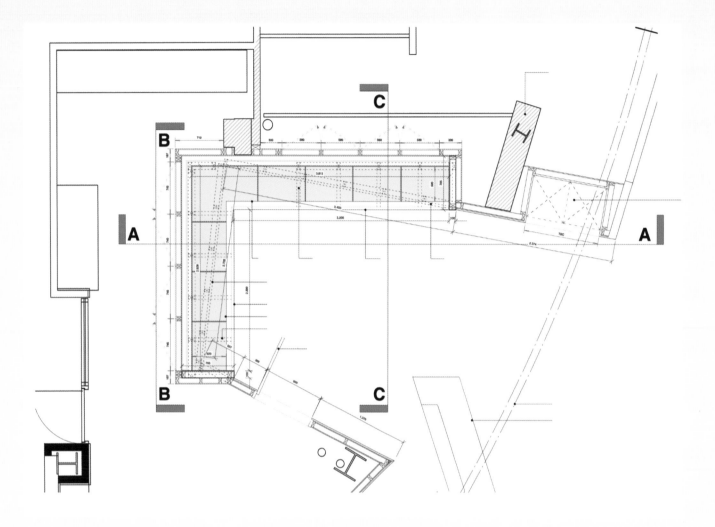

Because the individual spaces in this project are small and intricately detailed, the plan is drawn at a scale of 1:20. The drawing utilizes recognized conventions. The existing structure is hatched or outlined in black in order to distinguish it from the new, which is drawn in grey and includes more detail – showing construction information, such as the framing and the thickness of plasterboard sheeting. Blue colour-wash indicates glass shelving and is intensified in order to identify glass uprights.

Notes clarify the visual information, and are categorized into those in upper case explaining the significance of lines, and those in lower relating to the specification and construction of individual elements. Notes, while set apart from the drawn information of necessity, are close

enough to make a comprehensible connection with it.

The plan also shows the location of the sections via section lines, and these provide further general information about specification and vertical dimensions. The letters identifying them are black to give them prominence on the sheet.

A generic detail, such as this glass connection, need only be identified by word. It is drawn full size to allow space for the legible addition of notes.

Notes on the sections relate almost exclusively to individual elements and follow the lower-case convention. Those elements that require further explanation are drawn at a larger scale (1:5), and their locations on other drawings are indicated on the section with a red circle. It

is particularly worth observing the use of tone and colour on both drawings, distinguishing new work from old and identifying the most visually insubstantial material: glass.

Opposite

This 1:20 scale plan uses recognized conventions to illustrate a small, detailed space.

Below

This section for the same project uses blue tints to indicate glass. Areas that are also shown in greater detail in further drawings are circled in red. These are both common conventions.

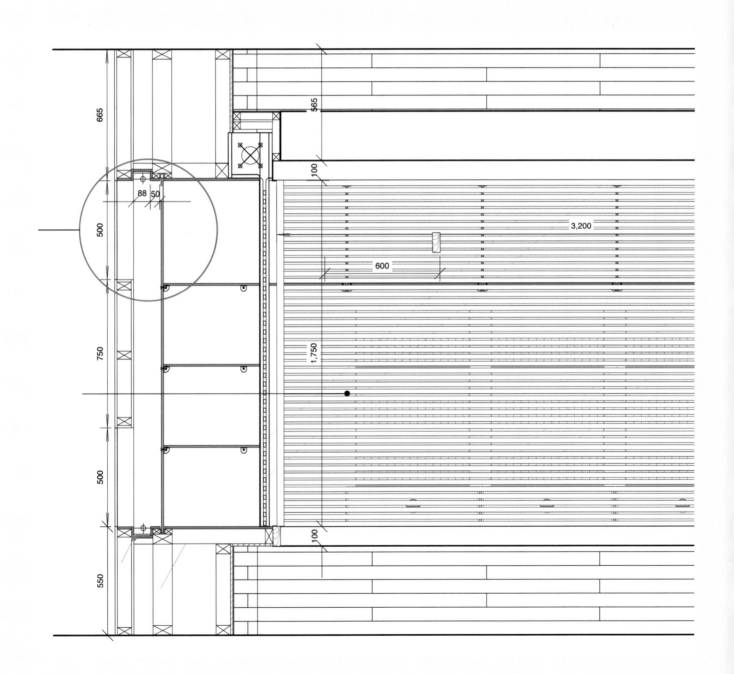

The scale of details created on computer may be inflated on-screen during development to be examined at full size – or larger, if required – in order to give an accurate appreciation of the sizes of the elements involved, and then automatically reduced to a more concise scale for distribution. Written notes may be added at typing speed, and amended, without the clumsy complications of stencils or the potential misinterpretation of handwriting.

Because computer drawings may be developed in separately saved layers, it is now more feasible to produce drawings specifically for individual trades and specialisms. While it was once expedient to use one drawing to communicate information about a number of separate activities, it is now as easy to produce a dedicated drawing for each and to deliver instructions with focused clarity. This not only reduces the likelihood of potential errors but, by providing a trade-specific drawing, eases the individual specialist's job and eliminates the uncertainty that can result from complex composite instructions.

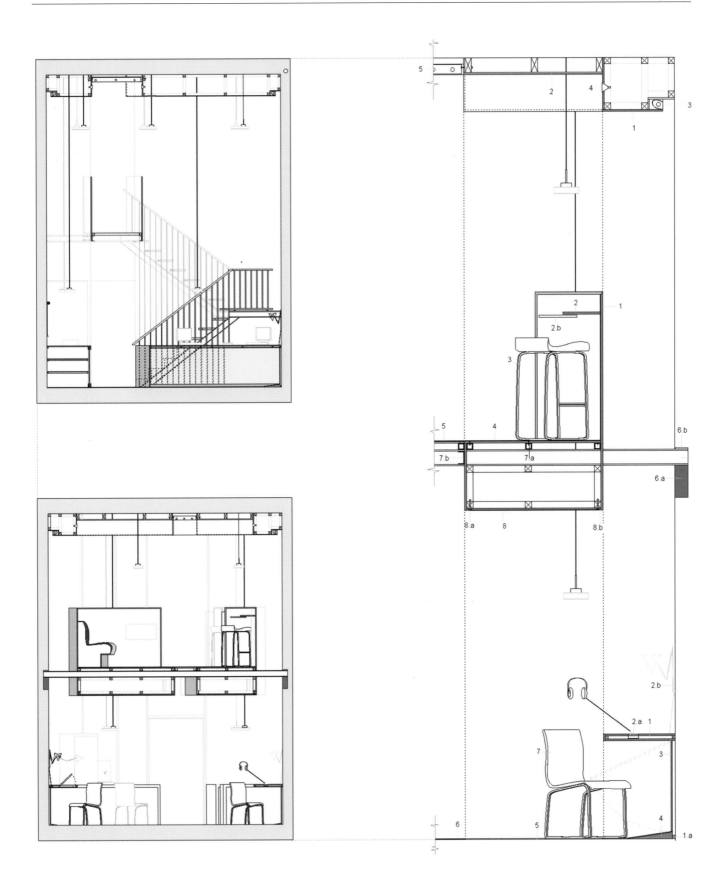

Annotation

There is a vocabulary and grammar particular to writing notes on drawings that should be mastered and adhered to. Technical terms and phrases should be learnt, because using the wrong word can seriously undermine credibility on site.

Notes should be brief: they should be phrases rather than sentences, and purely factual. They are instructions to the contractor, and so should not be explanations of aesthetic intentions or anticipated effects. Generally, they need to make three factual statements: they should name the material or the object to which they refer, they should state its size, and concisely describe the method of installing it (for example: '10 mm plywood screwed to 94 x 44 sw stud'). It is safe to assume that three such pieces of information should be added to every individual element within a detailed drawing. If one of them is unnecessary, that will be clearly evident and it may be omitted. If additional information is required, this is likely to be less obvious and, for all details, the designer needs to visualize the process of assembly and decide if it is comprehensively, but concisely, described in the notes. It should then be apparent if something needs to be added.

Right
Production drawings are almost inevitably covered with dimensions and notes. This potentially makes a drawing confusing to read, and the solution is often to put dimensions on the main drawing along with numbers referring to, in this case, the performance-specification notes, which are contained in the column on the right-hand side. Such notes are intended to ensure that the quality of the work carried out is satisfactory. It is worth reading the standard note in the top right corner that both puts responsibility for quality on the contractors and requires all decisions to be referred to the designers for approval.

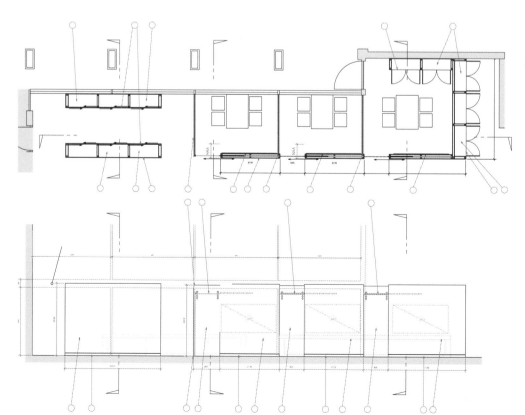

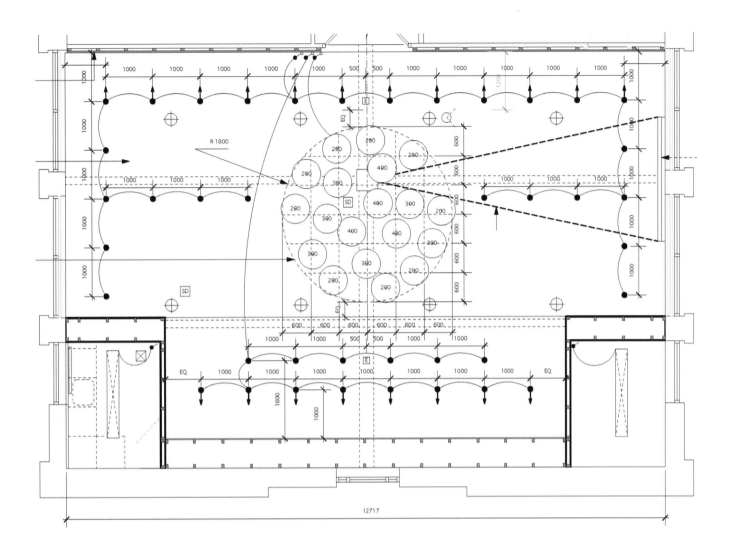

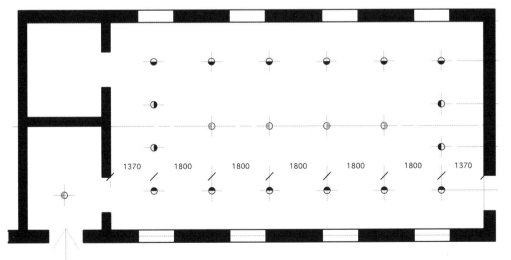

Left and above

The complexity of drawings depends on the complexity of the project. The plan above contains detailed specification, including the heights at which pendant lights will hang in different locations. That on the left has a less demanding information load: flush fittings need no height specification.

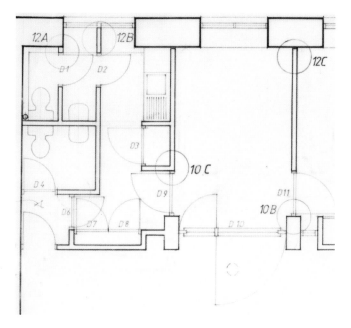

Numbering and cross-referencing

Production and detail drawings must be intelligently ordered, numbered and cross-referenced. Plans and sections constitute ways in which to communicate the overview of a project. They will show the precise locations and lengths of walls and other major elements in the case of a plan, and heights in the case of a section. When setting out dimensions, it is standard practice to relate measurements to significant existing points within the structure. Some generic specification information – such as materials for wall construction, and floor and wall finishes – should also be communicated on plans and sections. However, when very specific information about the materials and construction of, for example, a junction between a new wall and an existing structure is called for, then this should be drawn at a larger scale – and probably on another sheet. It is then standard practice to identify the location of that detailed condition, and to cross-reference it by giving it a unique number and by citing the sheet number on which it will appear (for example: 'detail C, drawing 53'). Other details, such as those for skirtings and architraves, which may have an application throughout a project need not have their locations specifically cited, but should also be numbered for efficient referencing during communication between designer and site workers.

Above
The circles indicate areas for which more detailed information has been produced. The accompanying number refers to the drawing on which this information is to be found and the letter identifies the relevant detail on that sheet. Doors are numbered, for example D1, so that each one's particular frame and ironmongery provisions may be specified on a separate drawing.

Below
The drawing's number is shown in bold type in the right hand corner and letters identifying details (which further amplify the designer's intention for the different conditions where new internal walls meet existing structure) are also emphasized.

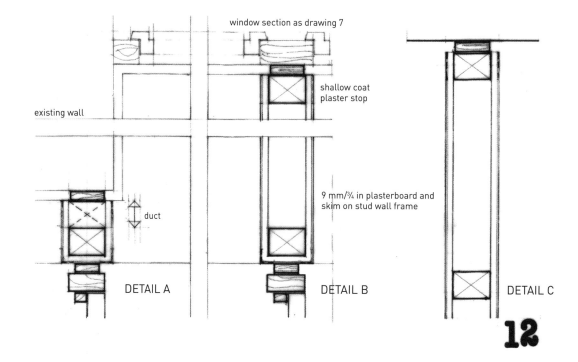

DETAIL A

DETAIL B

DETAIL C

window section as drawing 7

shallow coat plaster stop

9 mm/¾ in plasterboard and skim on stud wall frame

existing wall

duct

12

Amendments

Once a drawing has been issued, whether before tendering or after work has begun on site, it is not unusual for some changes to be necessary. Making such amendments once involved laborious erasing of pen and pencil lines, and this invariably resulted in deterioration of the drawing surface. Nowadays computer drawings may be changed leaving no trace left of the original error, but all those involved in the building operation need to be alerted to the fact that changes have been made and be made aware of what they are.

When changes have been made to all the appropriate drawings, they should be described verbally in an 'amendment box', usually a vertical column on the right-hand side of the drawing, be dated and given an identifying number or letter (for example: 'amendment C. relocation of office door').

The number of the sheet, or sheets, on which the amendment appears should then take on the letter or number of this last amendment as a suffix. For example, a drawing numbered 23B, because it has already been amended twice (A and B), will take the revised number 23C when amendment C is added. It is normal and efficient practice to issue a copy of the amended drawing to everyone involved in the construction process. All involved must be made aware of every change made because of the potential, sometimes unanticipated, impact on other activities on site.

Below

Table of revisions to accompany a production drawing. The letters on the left identify the individual amendments but will not appear on the drawing itself since written description should identify changes clearly. The right hand column records the date on which the revision is made and issued to contractors.

Revision	Details	Date
A	Site sizes applied. Feature wall amended. Fire escape reconfigured.	08 02 07
B	Fire safety symbols shown	21 02 07
C	Fire escape reconfigured. New furniture sizes shown. Builders' notes amended.	01 03 07
D	Fire escape corridor enlarged. Escape doors enlarged. Electrical note added.	30 03 07
E	Ramp between areas shown.	23 04 07
F	Fire door U valve and vision panel shown. Floor height difference accommodated.	03 05 07
G	Ceiling detail amended. Flooring rake relocated.	18 05 07
H	Dead end to fire escape reduced in depth.	23 05 07
J	Fire escape redirected.	01 06 07

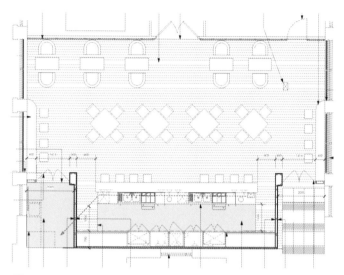

Above
The designer's drawing establishes layout and dimensions. Materials and practical requirements will be discussed with the contractor.

Collaborating with contractors

Contractors, particularly those responsible for highly specialist work, will frequently suggest simpler and cheaper ways of achieving the desired outcome, and if the designer is confident that the result will be aesthetically acceptable and will meet practical requirements, then there is every reason to accept the alternative offered. It is reasonable under these circumstances to ask contractors to provide a guarantee of quality, and perhaps a reduction in cost. Whether things go smoothly on site or not, if production drawings are comprehensive and sound then the project should proceed without friction because individual responsibilities will be clear and those involved will have confidence that the outcome will be satisfactory.

With specialist trades, such as furniture manufacture, it is common practice to select a contractor on the strength of a quotation based on drawings, produced by the designer, which establish precisely the configuration and specification of finishes of the elements required but do not specify construction techniques. This is a recognition that a better and more economical job is likely to result if manufacturers are able to use the techniques most suited to their machinery. Such specialists will provide what are, in effect, their own detailed production drawings, and they should give these to the designer for approval before beginning the work. The designer will, in these circumstances, be primarily checking that there have been no changes that affect the aesthetic intention, because the specialists will take responsibility for practical performance.

A designer should not expect to know everything. As the individual ultimately responsible for the success of a project, it is more important for them to be able to bring an intelligent, critical eye to bear on its development in order to control the interaction between aesthetic intention and practical considerations.

Drawings should not set out to be complicated. However, this may be inevitable with intricately detailed interiors, when they must carry enough information to ensure that, with a number of contractors competing for the tender, the extent of the work and the quality of its execution is clearly stated, leaving no ambiguities that might lead to later disputes on site.

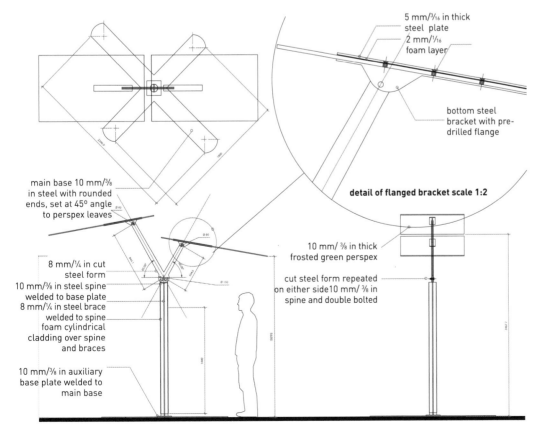

5 mm/³⁄₁₆ in thick
steel plate
2 mm/¹⁄₁₆
foam layer

bottom steel
bracket with pre-
drilled flange

detail of flanged bracket scale 1:2

main base 10 mm/³⁄₈
in steel with rounded
ends, set at 45° angle
to perspex leaves

10 mm/ ³⁄₈ in thick
frosted green perspex

cut steel form repeated
on either side10 mm/ ³⁄₈ in
spine and double bolted

8 mm/¹⁄₄ in cut
steel form
10 mm/³⁄₈ in steel spine
welded to base plate
8 mm/¹⁄₄ in steel brace
welded to spine
foam cylindrical
cladding over spine
and braces

10 mm/³⁄₈ in auxiliary
base plate welded to
main base

Above

The contractor's drawing sets
out the more detailed specialist
information for manufacturing.
It will be sent to the designer for
approval before production.

Left

While decisions about the
production of simple pieces of
furniture and equipment, such as
storage units and worktops, may
be left largely to the contractors
(with the proviso that they seek
approval for their decisions), it
is important when unfamiliar,
and probably unprecedented,
objects are proposed that they
are described in more detail.
Designers should, however, still
discuss final production decisions
with the selected fabricator, who is
likely to be able to bring specialist
knowledge to bear on final
decision-making.

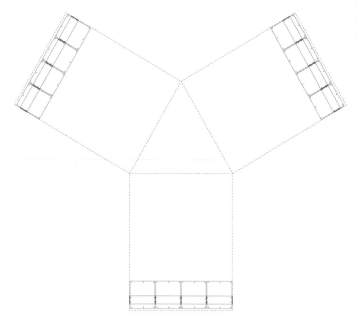

Construction sequence

The following drawings were made in order to describe the construction of a display area within a museum. While the structure was comparatively simple to construct, it was difficult to understand the form from the plan and section drawings. Consequently, three-dimensional images were made to clarify the designer's intention. Had the drawings for this project been made manually it would have been possible – indeed, essential – to provide the same information about profiles and construction techniques, but extremely difficult and time-consuming to produce the three-dimensional illustrations.

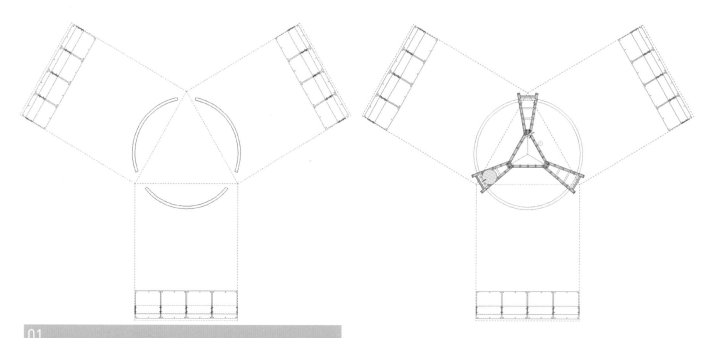

01
Each drawing is made in 'layers', and these are overlaid sequentially to produce finished, composite drawings. Each layer may subsequently be amended without elaborate redrawing of the whole.

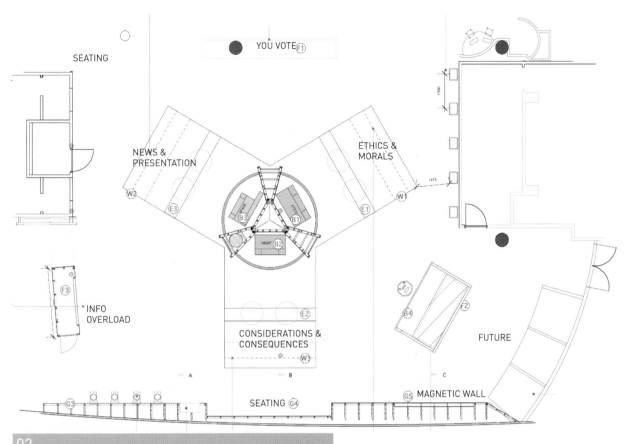

SEATING

YOU VOTE F1

NEWS &
PRESENTATION

ETHICS &
MORALS

W2

E3

B3 B1

HEART B2

F3

INFO
OVERLOAD

W1

E1

B4 F2

FUTURE

E2

CONSIDERATIONS &
CONSEQUENCES

W3

A   B   C

G3   SEATING G4   G5 MAGNETIC WALL

02
The first plan shows the three-sided element in the context of other exhibition structures.

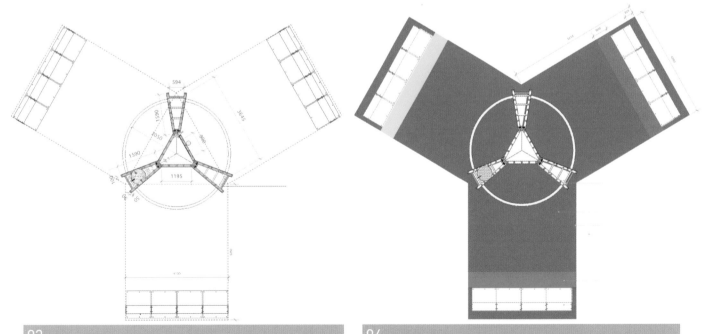

594

1590

2050

1590

1195

3645

03
The second gives critical dimensions and describes the principles of construction and finishes.

04
Variant drawings may be produced specifically for different trades.

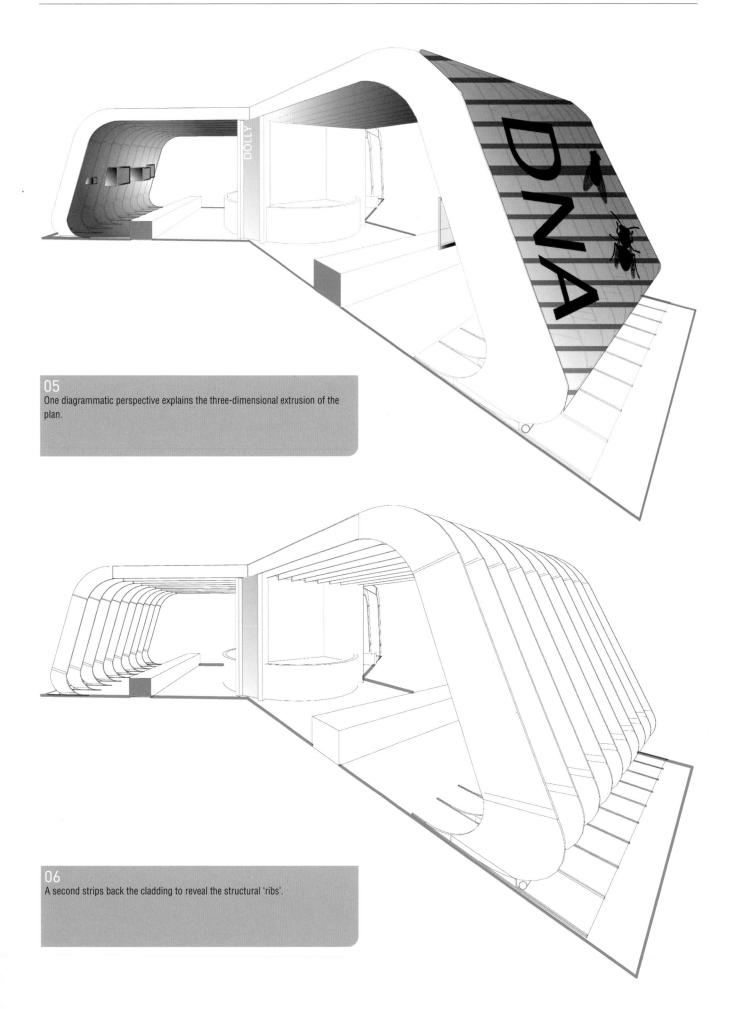

05
One diagrammatic perspective explains the three-dimensional extrusion of the plan.

06
A second strips back the cladding to reveal the structural 'ribs'.

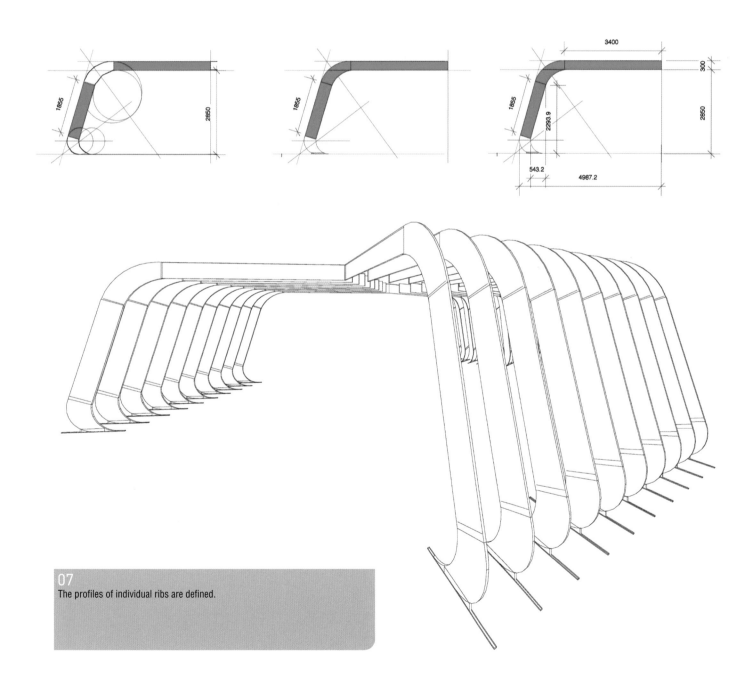

07
The profiles of individual ribs are defined.

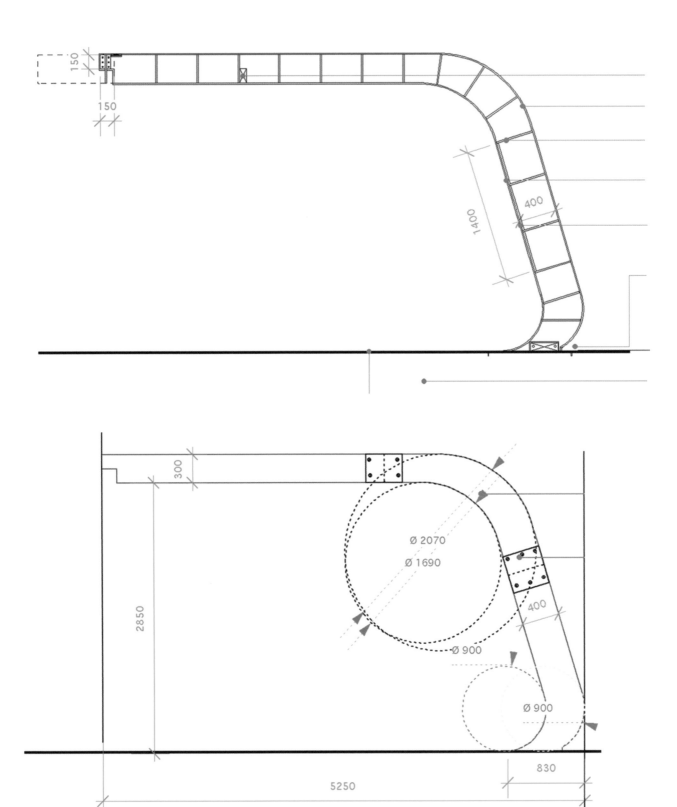

This composite A3 drawing communicates the remaining information about
dimensions and fixings, augmented by explanatory three-dimensional diagrams.

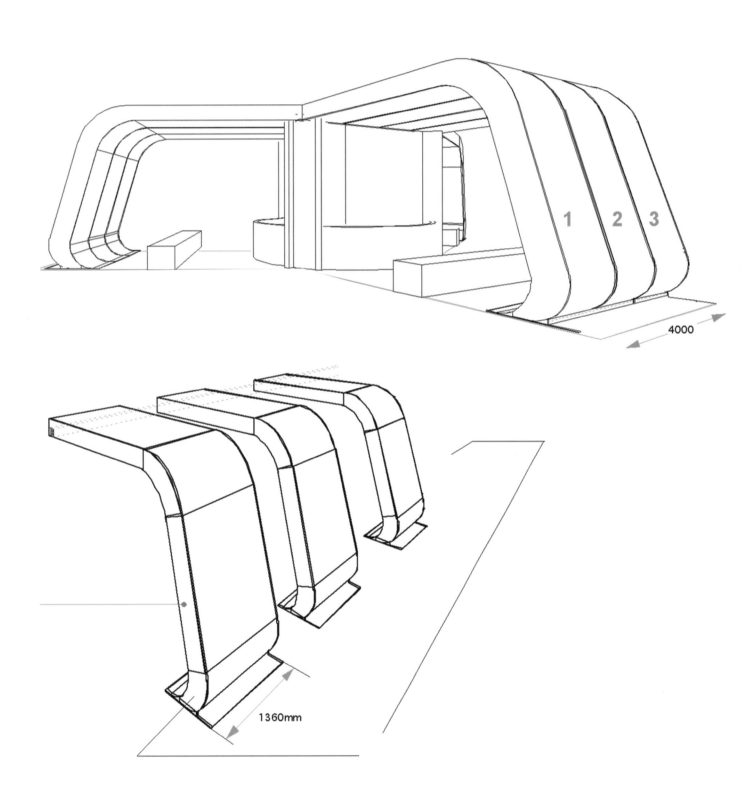

1 2 3

4000

1360mm

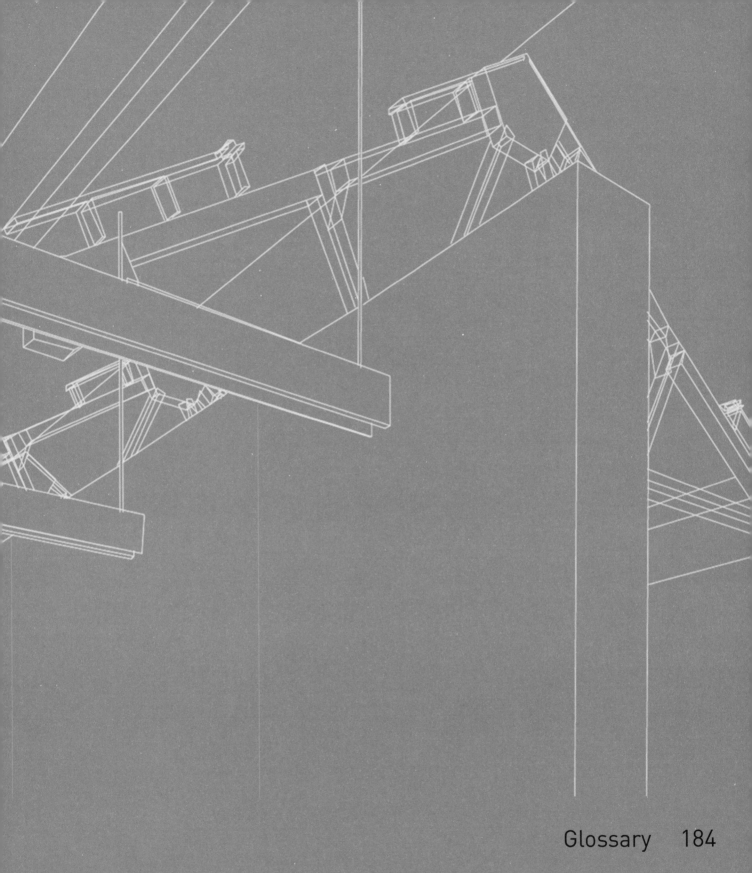

Glossary

There are a number of words relating to the practice of drawing within interior design that are more or less understood by everyone but are open – and vulnerable – to individual interpretation. Ambiguities are further complicated by words that have necessarily been imported from new technologies. For the sake of clarity, it is worth defining a few of the more crucial words and phrases used in this book.

Drawing

A dictionary definition of a drawing is '*a picture or plan made by means of lines on a surface, especially one made with a pencil or pen: a sketch or outline*'. Such a definition held true for interior designers until the advent of the computer and more or less remains true if the computer is added to the list of drawing instruments.

The same dictionary defines the activity of drawing as '*the art of making drawings, draughtsmanship*' and this applies very satisfactorily to interior design. So, while the word will continue to trail the idea of the hand-made behind it, it will serve very well to categorize the activities that concern us here.

The word 'drawing' can be used to describe everything, from a perfunctory scribble to the most highly refined artefact. It can describe something that is abstract, impressionistic, realistic or technical, which may be freehand, made with technical instruments, or made with computers: all are graphic artefacts, created with the single intention of creating and bringing to completion an interior design project.

Of course a drawing may also refer to the sheet of paper on which a number of individual drawings, however generated, are collected, usually for distribution to those involved in the process of commissioning, creating and constructing an interior project. Everything that emanates from an interior designer's studio, other than a letter, tends to be described as a drawing and that convention is accepted in this book.

Drawings may be further classified by the following terms:

Digital drawing
Made using a computer.

Freehand drawing
Refers to a drawing made entirely without technical instruments and judged by eye, or to a drawing for which the essential delineation is made by instruments but which is finished by hand.

Image
A drawing, primarily three-dimensional, created on a computer.

Manual drawing
Made by hand, with or without technical instruments.

Model
There are two types of model:
- **Physical** or **'real'**: a three-dimensional representation, made to scale. A physical construction as opposed to a drawing.
- **Digital** or **virtual**: a three-dimensional, computer-generated **image** or **drawing**, usually rendered to achieve a high degree of realism.

Rendering
A drawing, usually three-dimensional and made either on a computer or by hand, which uses colour and tone.

Technical drawing
There are two types of technical drawing:
- Made to scale, on a computer with appropriate drawing software, or by hand, using the traditional range of instruments: a scale ruler, set squares, compasses, pencils or pens.
- A drawing, usually made to scale but occasionally freehand, made to communicate technical information.

Visualization
An accurate three-dimensional, usually colour-rendered, representation of an interior, once hand made with technical instruments but now more likely to be computer-generated.

Index

Page numbers in *italics* refer to picture captions

Picture credits

1 Hyun Hee Kang
2–3 Olga Valentinova Reid
4–5 Olga Valentinova Reid
6 top left Louise Martin
6 top right Ali Stewart
6 right Jason Milne
7 Olga Valentinova Reid
8 left Jason Milne
8 right Michelle Lillejhem
9 top left Simon Capriotti
9 top right Stuart Gordon
9 bottom Emma Wynn
10 top left Karen Hamilton
10 left Neil Owen
10 right Stephen Noon
11 Olga Valentinova Reid
12 top left and right Richard Smith
12 bottom left and right Olga Valentinova Reid
13 top left and right Richard Smith
13 bottom left and right Olga Valentinova Reid
14 left Robert Harvey
14 top right Olga Valentinova Reid
14 bottom right Richard Smith
15 top left and right Yoon Si Yoon
15 bottom left and right Roseann Macnamara
16 top left and top right Claire Roebuck
16 centre left and centre right Olga Valentinova Reid
16 bottom left and bottom right Louise Martin
18–19 Yoshi Sugimoto
20 top Nathan Napier
20 bottom James Kaney
22–23 Drew Plunkett
28–33 Olga Valentinova Reid
34 left Drew Plunkett
34 right Zaheed Khalid
35 top Paula Murray
35 bottom Zoe Tucker
36 Patrick Macklin
37–43 Drew plunkett
44 top Amanda Youlden
44 bottom Drew Plunkett
45 Robert Millar
46 left Angela Pignatelli
46 right Jason Milne
47 left Paul Revie
47 right Drew Plunkett
50–51 Tess Syder

52 top John Gigli
52 bottom Vivien Maxwell
53 top Vivien Maxwell
53 bottom Amanda Youlden
54 left Robert Millar
54 right Gina Leith
55 Lucy Galloway
56–57 Robert Millar
58–59 Paula Murray
60 Jason Milne
61 top Drew Plunkett
61 bottom Louise Martin
62 top Arlene MacPhail
62 bottom Olga Valentinova Reid
63 Nicky Bruce
64–65 Drew Plunkett
66–67 Emma Franks
68–69 Claire Probert
70–71 Jason Milne
72 Alex Erikson
73 top Chris Matthews
73 centre left and centre right Zaheed Khalid
73 bottom Nathan Napier
74 Craig Tinney
75 top Helen Davies
75 bottom Val Clugston
76–77 Kevin Maclachlan
78 top Grant Morrison
78 bottom Hyun Hee Kang
79 Paula Murray for Graven Images
80–81 Jason Milne for Inspire Design
82 left Joe Lynch
82 right Lisa Donati
83 top Ellie McCallum
83 bottom Lara Cholbi
84 top Louise Martin
84 centre left and right Jason Milne
84 bottom Nicky Bruce
85 Jason Milne for DMG Design
86–87 Olga Valentinova Reid with The Curious Group
88–89 Olga Valentinova Reid
90–91 James Connor
92 Hyun Hee Kang
93–95 Jason Milne for Contagious
96–97 Nomad
98 top Arka
98 bottom James Connor
99 top Jason Milne for Contagious
99 bottom Melba Beetham
100 Drew Plunkett
101 Jennifer Laird
102 top Louise Martin
102 bottom Gillian Polonis

103 left **Robert Harvey**
103 right **Drew Plunkett**
104–105 **Olga Valentinova Reid**
106 top **James Connor**
106 bottom **Ezra Paris**
107 **Ezra Paris**
108 top **Petra Probstner**
108 bottom **Simon Capriotti**
109 top **Jennifer Laird**
109 bottom **Stephen Noon**
110 **Somya Singh**
111 **Kathryn Taggart**
112 top left and right **Emma Wynn**
112 bottom left **Julie McFadden**
112 bottom right **Sharon Kane**
113 **Morena Marchetti**
114 top **Martyn Cotter**
114 bottom **Api Tunshakul**
115 top **Aminah Habib**
115 bottom **Emma Campbell**
116 top **Oliver Shields**
116 bottom **Gillian Polonis**
117 top **Jenni Riach**
117 bottom **Sharon Kane**
118 **Robbie Crocker**
119 **Api Tunshakul**
120 left **Kathryn Taggart**
120 right **Monika Gromek**
121 top **Stephen Noon**
121 bottom **Julie McFadden**
122 **Elliott Rochford**
123 top **Claire Roebuck**
123 bottom **Hok Chun Chau**
124 **Rachel Glue**
125 **Petra Probstner**
126 **Lisa Donati**
127 top **Lisa Donati**
127 bottom **James Connor**
128–129 **Olga Valentinova Reid**
130 left **Paula Murray for Graven Images**
131 top **Carolyn Maxwell**
131 centre and bottom left **Scott Mason**
131 bottom right **Rachel Munro**
132 **Christine Myers**
133 left **Ross Burgoyne**
133 right **Richard Smith**
134 **Annmarie Murphy**
135 **Gillian Polonis**
136–137 **Karen Hamilton**
138 top **James Connor**
138 bottom left **Anna Montgomery**
138 bottom right **Lisa Donati**
139 top **Jenni Riach**

139 bottom **Olga Valentinova Reid**
140 **Xander Gardner**
141 top and centre **Hannah Parker**
141 bottom **Jenny Banks**
142 **Lisa Donati**
143 **Lara Cholbi**
144 top **Olga Valentinova Reid**
144 right **Laure Derolez**
145 **Jill Rodger**
146 **Angus Shepherd**
147 top **James Kaney**
147 bottom **Nathan Napier**
150–152 **James Kaney**
153 top **Stephen Noon**
153 bottom **Xander Gardner with Digger Nutter**
154–155 **Petra Probstner**
156–158 **Olga Valentinova Reid**
159 **Drew Plunkett**
160–161 **Sam Booth**
162 left **Petra Probstner**
162 right **Jason Milne**
163 **Jason Milne**
164 **Nomad**
165 **Jason Milne with Contagious**
166–167 **Martin Cotter with Graven Images**
169 **Petra Probstner**
170 **Nomad**
171 **Jason Milne with Contagious**
172 **Drew Plunkett**
174 **Jason Milne with Contagious**
175 top **Elmwood Joinery**
175 bottom **Nomad**
176–180 **Olga Valentinova Reid**

Author's acknowledgements

I am grateful to everyone who contributed to this book, but particularly to Digger Nutter who introduced so many to the fundamentals of digital imaging, to Jason Milne, whose virtuosity across media proves that great drawing depends on the maker and not the medium, and to Olga Valentinova Reid for her exploration of the far reaches of digital imaging and her generosity in creating so many drawings especially for the book.